Gesture

Gesture

A SLIM GUIDE

Lauren Gawne

Great Clarendon Street, Oxford, OX2 6DP,
United Kingdom

Oxford University Press is a department of the University of Oxford.
It furthers the University's objective of excellence in research, scholarship,
and education by publishing worldwide. Oxford is a registered trade mark of
Oxford University Press in the UK and in certain other countries

Published in the United States of America by Oxford University Press
198 Madison Avenue, New York, NY 10016, United States of America

British Library Cataloguing in Publication Data

Data available

Library of Congress Control Number: 2024951304

ISBN 9780192855077
ISBN 9780192855084 (pbk.)

DOI: 10.1093/9780198951377.001.0001

Printed and bound by
CPI Group (UK) Ltd, Croydon, CR0 4YY

Cover image: artwork by Lucy Maddox

The manufacturer's authorised representative in the EU for product safety is
Oxford University Press España S.A. of El Parque Empresarial San Fernando de Henares, Avenida
de Castilla, 2 – 28830 Madrid (www.oup.es/en or
product.safety@oup.com). OUP España S.A. also acts as importer into Spain
of products made by the manufacturer.

*This book is dedicated to the memory of Barbara F. Kelly.
I am forever grateful that she introduced me to Gesture Studies and I
miss her dearly as a mentor, colleague, and friend.*

Contents

Acknowledgements

Thanks to all of my colleagues with whom I have worked on research projects that sit within Gesture Studies; Suzy Styles, Kristine Hildebrandt, Kensy Cooperrider, Gretchen McCulloch, Jennifer Daniel, Alexander Robertson, Peta F. Freestone, and Jess Kruk. I get to write about the most interesting things with the most interesting people.

Thanks also to my colleagues at La Trobe University; I only had the space to propose and write this book thanks to having an ongoing job. Thank you to Adam Schembri, who set up the subject Language and Gesture when he was at La Trobe, and thanks to Gabrielle Hodge and Jess Kruk, who also taught the subject and made it all the better. Teaching this subject has been a joy, and I'm grateful to all the students who helped push me to explain and teach key concepts in Gesture Studies.

Thanks to all my Gesture Studies colleagues in the International Society for Gesture Studies. I love being part of a global network of researchers across disciplines and areas of interest and I'm grateful for all of the research that I get to draw on in this book. By far the biggest writing challenge I faced was whittling down citations and references when there is so much great work being done.

Thank you to Julia Steer from Oxford University Press for the chat at the International Congress of Linguists in Cape Town in 2019. What I thought was a casual chat about the Slim Guide series planted the seed for what would eventually be this book. At the other end of the project, thank you to Claire Gawne, who read early versions of each chapter and gave the kind of honest feedback only a sister can offer and thank you to Christine Gawne, who proofread the manuscript. Thanks also to Peta F. Freestone and Gretchen McCulloch for thoughtful comments on a later version of the book. Thanks also to Gretchen for the many chats along the way about writing, gesture, and lingcomm. Thanks to Vicki Sunter at OUP and Roopa Vineetha Nelson at Integra for their work on the production of this book, and to Kim Allen for the attentive copy editing. My thanks to Lucy Maddox for much of the art that features as figures in this book, including the wonderful front cover image inspired by the experimental stimulus video used in Gawne and Kelly (2014). Lucy draws the best hands.

Thanks to my friends and family, who were subjected to many anecdotes about whatever chapter I was working on at any given time. Thanks to my partner Andrew, for always being on board for the adventure.

Finally, thanks to Barb Kelly. Barb was so supportive of this book and I am so sad to not be able to share the final publication with her. My enthusiasm for Gesture Studies is all her fault. From her supervision of my honours thesis, to graduate supervision, collaborations, and supportive chats, she made me the researcher I am today, and it is for this reason this book is dedicated to her.

List of figures and tables

1

Introduction

Across the span of human existence, communication has predominantly been something that happens face to face. Writing is millennia old, but human language has been with us far longer. The role of the whole human in communication becomes evident when we pay attention to face-to-face communication. Alongside speech or sign, there are actions made with the human body. On close attention, a set of these actions appear to be intentionally communicative, and deeply integrated into the larger communicative system. These actions, or gestures, are the topic of this book. Whatever your specific interest, this guide provides a broad introduction to the ways we can make sense of the contribution gesture makes to human communication.

Observing gestures in your everyday environment may initially feel trivial, but can lead to big questions regarding the nature of gesture and its role in language, cognition, and culture. Why are some people better than others at pointing in the direction of distant objects and locations? Why do we gesture on the phone, when the person we are talking to cannot see us? And why do we have common names for some types of gestures, such as pointing, nodding, and thumbs up, but not for others? When I teach courses on gesture in communication there is always a session a few weeks into the course when my students tell me that they suddenly notice gestures, and their vital importance in interaction, everywhere. This is an unavoidable and delightful risk of studying gesture, and I hope you too begin to notice the small questions that emerge as you pay attention to the gestures around you. This book is intended to help you link these questions to bigger answers.

Gesture. Lauren Gawne, Oxford University Press. © Lauren Gawne (2025).
DOI: 10.1093/9780198951377.003.0001

Paying attention to gesture in communication means paying attention to the fuller context in which humans communicate. Gesture is absolute, in that every human community that has language also has gestures as part of that language. But gesture is also incredibly relative, in that it is far more heavily context dependent than linguistic elements of communication. A hand can be in the same configuration but have a variety of functions depending on context; an extended index finger could be used to point, or to represent the body of a person in the enactment of a story. This primacy of context means that, even with the most robust methods, the best approaches are those that show patience in the analysis and always centre the original data.

The last few decades have seen the blossoming of the field of Gesture Studies, as researchers from a wide range of disciplines seek a richer and more complete account of human communication. This book is intended to provide a broad introduction to current understandings of the nature and function of gesture as a feature of human communication. I have tried to write this book to be approachable regardless of your own experience or background.

Gesture studies across disciplines

The growing interest in gesture has been part of a larger trend in the last few decades of approaching human thought, language, and experience as fundamentally tied to the physical reality of embodied communication (Iverson and Thelen 1999). Work with this focus on 'embodiment' turns up in many of the disciplines and research traditions this book draws on. Each comes with their own methods of analysis and uses gestural evidence to advance a range of theories and debates.

Psychologists have used gesture to give insights into cognitive processing, observing how gestures provide evidence of imagistic thinking (McNeill 1992, 2005) and embodied schematic thinking (Kita et al. 2017). Linguists have used gesture to understand how people construct meaning in conversation (Kendon 2004), and to provide evidence that grammar has cognitive effects, such as with spatial directions (Haviland 2000). Anthropologists have analysed the role of gesture in human social interactions (Goodwin 2007), and as features of larger cultural ecologies (Morris et al. 1979). Researchers have also studied gesture to better understand theatre (Astington 2006), orchestral conducting (Poggi 2011), and creative arts (Campana et al. 2011). Understanding gesture is also foundational to the study of first and second language acquisition (Morgenstern and Goldin-Meadow 2021) and the development of more sophisticated parsing of multimodal speech in computer science (Trujillo et al. 2019).

Gesture Studies gains its strength from this dynamism of interdisciplinary research. There is no single preferred methodology or focus of study. Some researchers will focus on a particular type of gestures, while others will include gesture in a larger category of non-linguistic communication. In this book we will encounter both qualitative and quantitative methods across a range of experimental, corpus, and observational approaches. We will see that the field has attracted researchers from many disciplines, who work with various languages, both spoken and signed, in diverse contexts. Yet there is still much to be explored within Gesture Studies, and the opportunities about for students and researchers from many fields to incorporate gesture research within their own discipline. This slim guide provides a high-level introduction to the terminology and key areas of research within the field of Gesture Studies.

A brief note on terminology

Throughout this book I draw on examples from a range of languages to illustrate the role of gesture in human communication. This includes both spoken and signed languages. I discuss the relationship between gesture and signed language—which share a modality but have other differences—in Chapter 2. I use the term 'speaker' as a modality–agnostic pair part with 'addressee', although I use the term 'signer' when talking about specific signed language examples. I am yet to settle on a single, satisfying term that describes the relationship between gesture and the other elements of the spoken or signed language that it occurs with. The reason this is not entirely elegant is because people often use 'language' to refer to a subset of linguistic structures, but as we'll see language is more than that. In this book I will mostly talk about the relationship between the gestural and linguistic elements of communication. When I talk about the relationship of gesture and language, I do so with the approach that gesture is a component of language, and not separate from it. Overall, where possible I use the most generally agreed upon terminology across Gesture Studies research. The majority of terminology in this book is introduced in the next two chapters, where we discuss the structural properties and categories of gesture. There is a glossary of terminology at the end of the book. The field of Gesture Studies, like many areas of the social sciences, still has a strong focus on a small sub-set of the world's linguistic diversity. I have usually flagged what language(s) a study focuses on, but have taken to often leaving English unspecified because the repeition can become distracting and a little bit passive aggressive.

Outline of this book

There are two major sections of the book. The first is an introduction to key terms and features of gesture in Chapters 2 and 3. If you are thinking of analysing gesture in your own work, these chapters should provide the basis for approaching this task. The second half of the book uses this knowledge to look at the contribution of Gesture Studies in different contexts. These chapters draw on the terminology in Chapters 2 and 3, but you can jump straight into them and make use of the glossary of key terms at the back of the book.

In Chapter 2, we explore how gesture communicates meaning using a different structure to the linguistic systems of spoken and signed languages. The integration of speech and gesture is seen in their close temporal relationship, which holds across languages. This chapter also provides an introduction to the physiology of gesture, including the way we describe these bodily movements and the structure of how gestures are performed. In order to understand how the modern approach to gesture studies emerged, this chapter also provides a brief introduction to the history of the field. Chapter 3 provides an overview of major gesture categories that are used in the Gesture Studies literature.

In the second half of this book we look at how gesture provides insight into questions about human communication across cultures, across communicative contexts, across lifespans, and across history.

People across all languages and cultures gesture. Where there is language, there is gesture, and with this ubiquity we see some common features of gesture. That said, there are also distinctions in the use of gesture in different populations. In Chapter 4 we will explore some of the distinctions, including how the structure of gestures are shaped by the grammars of languages and the cultures of the people who speak them.

The importance of gesture in communication is seen in its usefulness for both the speaker and their audience. In Chapter 5, we will explore the ways gestures are shaped by speakers for their audience, as well as evidence for how gesture is useful for the speaker's thought processes. We will also look at the critical role of gesture in early language development and the relationship between gesture and learning a second language.

Chapter 6 looks at both the neurological and cognitive research to explore the relationship between gesture, movement, and language. We will look at both where gesture resides in the physical brain, and how it contributes to the processes of the mind.

Gesture is often discussed as an important feature in the evolutionary development of the linguistic skills of modern humans. Chapter 7 examines the debate on the role of gesture in language evolution. In addition, we explore work on gesture and communication for other animals and what this might tell us about the evolutionary origins of human language. As well as examining the history of human communication, we also look to the future. The second half of this chapter examines how gesture is being integrated into new technology.

The conclusion of each chapter is a summary overview of what was covered. If the Slim Guide format is not efficient enough for you, reading the conclusion of each chapter should provide you with an express introduction to the topic. The section of further reading and resources directs you to sources relevant to the chapter topics. Some of these provide a deeper dive into the topic, to help you take your next steps, while others provide a summary in a different format, including videos, podcasts, and popular scicomm. I hope these will be useful for further self-education, or alongside this book as curriculum resources in a formal educational setting.

It is worth noting that this book is not a systematic survey of the literature on gesture. I have tried to strike a balance between canonical works, neglected classics, and new work that showcases the potential future directions for Gesture Studies. I have also attempted to provide examples that draw on a variety of languages, across both the spoken and signed modalities.

Gesture studies is for everyone

I have used part of this introduction to advocate for the broad inter-disciplinary contribution that the study of gesture can make to our understanding of human communication. I want to return to this point here, because the interdisciplinary nature of Gesture Studies is one of the greatest attributes of this field of study, and it is one of the things that drew me to the study of gesture.

As a linguist, I believe that an account of human language that does not include gesture is an incomplete account. I also believe that some basic training in the nature of gesture is all that is needed to begin to incorporate observation and analysis of gesture into your own research or teaching programme. The study of gesture is not the domain of one specific discipline, a fact that is incredibly liberating. In my own work, I have drawn on gesture to explore a range of topics, including the way people perceive gestures (Gawne et al. 2010), how Syuba speakers in Nepal use gesture in narratives (Gawne 2018, 2021), the cross-cultural diversity of emblems (Freestone et al. 2023; Gawne and Cooperrider 2024), and the way the relationship between gesture and speech provides insights into the relationship between emojis and text (Gawne and McCulloch 2019). I have taught undergraduate subjects that provide an introduction to the study of gesture, and incorporated gesture research into teaching for a range of other subjects.

I remember when I first learnt about the field of Gesture Studies, in a lecture in one of the final subjects of my undergraduate degree. In one of the final lectures of my degree, Barb Kelly introduced me to the world of Gesture Studies with her trademark infectious enthusiasm. After that lecture I changed my graduation plans, and signed up for an honours year to study gesture. Part of the motivation for writing this book is that I wish that my undergraduate self had been able to pick up *Gesture: A Slim Guide* and dive straight into this fascinating interdisciplinary topic.

Conclusion

Gesture is an integral part of human communication, but one that has not always received a great deal of attention in academic research until relatively recently. The growth of the field of Gesture Studies has resulted in research from across a range of disciplines that highlights the important role that gesture plays in human interaction. An understanding of gesture is relevant to anyone who looks at human communication, and Gesture Studies is a highly interdisciplinary field that includes work from researchers in psychology, anthropology, linguistics, primatology, and more, and touches on interaction in varied domains including first and second language acquisition, artistic performance, and online interaction. This book provides an introduction to the key features and common categories of gesture, and its relationship to signed and spoken languages. We then look at how gesture can be studied from a variety of perspectives, including cultural variation, context of use, acquisition of gesture and language, gesture and the brain, and the origins and future of gesture in communication.

Further reading and resources

There are three books that are canonical and much cited resources in Gesture Studies. They were written by two scholars who made key contributions to the formalization of Gesture Studies as a field of research: David McNeill's two books, *Hand and Mind: What Gestures Reveal about Thought* (1992) and *Gesture and Thought* (2005), and Adam Kendon's *Gesture: Visible Action as Utterance* (2004). These books are key summaries of the approaches taken by two of the most influential scholars in the field of Gesture Studies. You will find at least one of these works cited in almost any Gesture Studies publication, and for good reason, Kendon's work laid the foundations for the understanding of the cultural and social value of gesture, and McNeill formalized much of the terminology of the field in his focus on the cognitive integration of gesture and language.

2

Gesture as an object of study

Gesture is the intentional communicative movement of the body, most notably the hands, usually in the context of spoken or signed language. Gesture is closely integrated with speech, but it has its own unique role in relation to other features of language. In this chapter we explore how gesture communicates meaning using context-dependent and imagistic features. It is these features that make gestures distinct in both spoken and signed language systems. Signed languages may share the manual modality with gesture, but have a very different structure. The integration of speech and gesture as part of a larger system is seen in their close temporal relationship. To understand the role of gesture in communication we have to understand the shape that gestures can take, and how people make use of the gesture space. Finally, in order to understand how the modern approach to gesture studies emerged, this chapter also provides a brief introduction to the history of the field, tracing the literature from ancient Greek writing on rhetoric, to nineteenth-century anthropology, and twentieth-century psychology and linguistics.

Gesture and moving the body

Not every movement of the body is a gesture. Gestures form part of our intentional communicative system, alongside and as part of language. Given how little attention we often pay to gesture, as speakers and addressees, it is worth clarifying specifically what we mean by intentional, and what other types of movements gestures contrast with.

Gesture. Lauren Gawne, Oxford University Press. © Lauren Gawne (2025).
DOI: 10.1093/9780198951377.003.0002

An unavoidable physiological response, such as a sneeze, is not a part of the gestural system in the way a gesture like pointing is (although a performed sneeze can be co-opted into the gesture repertoire if I am telling a story about seasonal allergies). Gestures are also generally considered to be distinct from actions that involve interacting with objects, so flipping a pancake in a frying pan would be an action, but acting out the same action while telling someone about how great you are at making pancakes would be a gesture. Similarly, touching your own body with self-grooming actions, from brushing back hair, to nail biting or absent-mindedly scratching behind your ear, are generally not treated as gestures, but mimicking those actions for a story would be. This distinction between gestures and other actions is because gestures are representing actions or items in the speech context rather than the physical context. The line is not always as clear as those examples; in an analysis of how people interact at an archaeological dig Goodwin (2007) illustrated the way that tools were used as part of the gesturing body. In Goodwin's work, we see how archaeologists working on the excavation of items at a prehistoric village used trowels to point at features of their work, or drew lines into the ground to indicate points of common focus.

Gesture is usually considered to be distinct from posture and gaze because of the way it is tightly aligned with the linguistic system. This is not to say that phenomena such as gaze do not contribute to communication, there has been a lot of research demonstrating the importance of eye gaze in regulating discourse (Goodwin 1980; Emmorey et al. 2008b; Brône et al. 2017). The way we hold the whole body also signals our relationship to the other participants in an interaction. What makes gesture distinct from these other features of interaction is the specific role it plays in formulating linguistic utterances. Of course, gesture researchers know as well as anyone that we ignore the full context of interaction at our peril, and understanding the role of gesture often includes considering these other features of interaction as well.

Communicatively intentional movement is a key feature of gesture, however there are still a variety of communicative movements we can do, which have different properties. One category is the gestures that we make alongside speech, which are often almost incomprehensible if we do not know what someone is saying alongside them. Because of their close relationship with speech, these are known as co-speech gestures (sometimes also referred to as gesticulations in the literature). We will look at common types of co-speech gesture in Chapter 3. In contrast, signed languages use the same modality but exist as full languages with no need of the verbal channel at all. These two uses of the body are at the extreme ends of what we do communicatively. McNeill (1985, 1992, 2005) visualized gesture and signed languages as being at the end points of a continuum, with other phenomena in between. There are also several properties that change as we move along the continuum, which are represented in Figure 1.

Co-Speech Gestures → Pantomime → Emblems → Signed Language

less structure	→	more structure
fewer linguistic properties	→	more linguistic properties
speech necessary	→	speech not necessary

Figure 1 The gesture continuum
Source: Based on McNeill (1992: 37)

Between these two ends, we have some other useful demarcated points that illustrate different uses of the body for communication. The first is pantomime, where basic gestural actions can come to have limited, stable meanings. This might happen in a game of charades, where miming the action of putting up an umbrella might refer to the film *Singing in the Rain* in one round, and Rihanna's song *Umbrella* in another. Sometimes these pantomimed actions can stabilize into a functional communicative system, essentially moving further along the continuum towards the signed language end of things.

The other demarcated stop on the gesture continuum is for emblems. Emblems are those gestures that do not need speech to exist, because they have a fixed form–meaning relationship for a community (Gawne and Cooperrider 2024). This includes gestures such as 'thumbs up', 'ok', and an affirmative head nod. While they have a stable meaning, and some word-like behaviours, they do not exist in a larger linguistic paradigm in the same way as words and signs. Emblems are by no means universal, but emblem gestures can exist in cultural areas larger than a single language. We return to this cultural variation in emblem gestures in Chapter 4.

By placing these different communicative uses of the body on a continuum in this way, McNeill illustrates interrelated factors that change across these different phenomena. The first is, as the continuum moves from left to right, we see an increase in structure and linguistic properties. In a signed language, signs have stable meanings, and need to be made in correct ways and in grammatical order. In contrast, if I gesture about the size of a tiny kitten, it does not matter if I use one hand, or two, or how I hold my hand. As a result, the corresponding observation is that the necessity of the verbal speech stream is reduced for signed languages. You do not need the verbal channel to say 'small cat' because the signs are saying it, while with gesture it is likely to not be apparent I'm gesturing about a small cat without the accompanying speech. Co-speech gestures and signed languages are so distinct in the way they use the body that signed languages, like spoken language, employ co-speech gestures (Hodge and Johnston 2014). To better understand the difference between gesture and language, let us examine the structural features of language, and how gesture is so distinct.

Gesture and language

Languages share a common set of features that allow us to distinguish 'language' from other communicative systems—such as animal communication, music, and computer code. These have been most famously summarized as Hockett's design features of language (Hockett 1960). Hockett's feature set has been expanded and challenged over time, but includes useful insights into what makes language the flexible and structured system that it is. Gestures do not share the structural features of language. This is advantageous, because it allows the two streams to work together as a larger communicative system. David McNeill has dedicated a significant amount of work to considering the different structural properties of language and gesture (McNeill 1992, 2005). This section uses his work as the basis for our exploration of the structural differences between gestures and speech, while also making clear the parallels with Hockett's design features of language.

There are four contrastive properties that distinguish language and gesture (McNeill 1992: 41). These are summarized in Table 1, followed by more detail in the sections below.

Table 1 Summary of the properties of gesture and speech

Properties of language	Properties of co-speech gesture
Hierarchical and analytic	Global and synthetic
Combinatoric	Non-combinatoric
Context-independent	Context-sensitive
Standards of form	No standards of form

One important thing to remember is that properties of language are not modality specific, but include both spoken and signed language. It is also possible to consider a more expanded definition of gestures that include verbal forms (Grenoble et al. 2014) or emojis (Gawne and McCulloch 2019).

Hierarchical and analytic/Global and synthetic

Language is built from multiple layers of structure where smaller units combine to make larger units of meaning. Languages have handshapes or sounds (phonemes), which combine into parts of words (morphemes), words, and sentences. These structures that build into flexible combinations are what make language hierarchical, and the fact that we can see and decompose these structures is what makes it analytical. The analytical nature is 'discreteness' for Hockett, while the hierarchical nature is Hockett's 'duality of patterning'. Gesture does not build meaning from this kind of structure. Instead, meaning is derived from the position of the body and limbs as a whole. The fact that there are no hierarchies allows meaning to be presented in a way that is global, and the inability to pull a gesture apart into smaller meaningful units is what makes it synthetic.

Combinatoric/Non-combinatoric

The hierarchical and analytical structure of language means that units can be combined in endless variation. This is the other key element of Hockett's 'duality of patterning'. We can easily attach a negative morpheme to a particular word in a sentence. In contrast, a negating gesture such as a headshake, scopes over the utterance more generally.

Context-independent/Context-sensitive

We can use language to talk about things that are happening outside of our immediate experience, whether that is physically or temporally (Hockett's 'displacement'). In contrast, gestures are far more context-sensitive. An extended index finger might be a pointing gesture, or it may be used to act out the ticking hand of a clock. This context-sensitivity is an empirical observation, not an anecdotal 'just so'; Feyereisen, Van de Wiele, and Dubois (1988) asked people to watch videos of speech and gesture with and without sound, and unsurprisingly found that a lot of the meaningful information in the gesture was only interpretable in the context where speech was audible.

Standards of form/No standards of form

Languages have utterances that speakers consider to be grammatically well-formed. Changing the initial /d/ in 'dog' to another sound would create a different word (such as 'cog' or 'hog'). This is part of the 'arbitrariness' of language in Hockett's design features. The smallest units of language do not necessarily carry meaning, but build into symbols that have meaning in specific combinations. Co-speech gestures, in contrast, are not required to meet standards of form. There are cultural conventions, for example your culture may have a preferred hand or finger used for pointing, but speakers can, and often do, manipulate this in context. Returning to the gesture continuum, this is a large part of why 'emblem' gestures are considered to be distinct from the categories of co-speech gestures. Emblem gestures are conventionalized signs, and therefore do have a standard form; rotate a thumbs up and you have a thumbs down. Place the middle finger upright instead of the thumb and you have a very different gesture indeed.

Central to understanding the relationship between gesture and language is understanding that gesture and language bring together different properties to create a rich, multimodal form of language. The very different properties of each element of multimodal communication mean that it is somewhat of a fool's errand to attempt to quantify exactly what percentage or proportion of meaning is being contributed in either channel (although that has not stopped some from trying, as Beattie (2016: 26–34) notes). Understanding the contribution of each element depends on the context and the content of a particular interaction.

Gesture and signed languages

So far we have distinguished gestures from languages, including signed languages. It is important to be very clear that all languages, regardless of modality, share features of structure that distinguish them from co-speech gestures (Marschark 1994). While being very clear on this primary point, it is worth specifically discussing the relationship between gestures and signed languages because of their shared modality.

Signed languages are often described as 'visual-spatial' languages. Spoken languages make use of the speech stream, which is essentially and unavoidably linear; we have to articulate the word for the subject of a sentence at a different point in time to the word for the object, because speech is constrained by the flow of air and movement of vocal articulators. Signed languages are articulated in three-dimensional space, and a proficient signer can draw on this resource to create utterances that make rich use of the visual and spatial properties of a signed language.

There are many signed languages around the world. Glottolog currently lists 227 documented signed languages (Hammarström et al. 2024). Signed languages do not necessarily follow spoken language histories or borders; American Sign Language (ASL) is actually related to French Sign Language (LSF), rather than British Sign Language (BSL), because it was French educators who brought their methods to the USA. There are also many regional or village signed languages, especially in areas with high percentages of deaf community members, such as Kata Kolok in Bali, Indonesia, and Al-Sayyid Bedouin Sign Language (ABSL) in the Negev desert of southern Israel.

Some communities have signed languages that are used in parallel to the local spoken language(s). These alternate sign systems have been documented in Australia (Kendon 1988; Green and Wilkins 2014) and North America (Mallery 1881/1972; Farnell 1995). There might be some deaf community members who use them, or they may serve particular functions for hunting, or if there is speech avoidance in mourning or other ritual avoidance (such as speaking to a son-in-law). Often it is a combination of multiple functions, with the alternate sign system also being integrated into the gestural repertoire of speaking members of the community.

As well as fully linguistic signed languages, there are also contexts where signed communication can arise, usually where the spoken modality is not a viable option. This includes basic systems such as the underwater hand sign conventions for scuba divers, umpire signals in organized sport, and systems used in noisy industrial contexts (Harrison 2014). In the context of scuba hand signals, a raised thumb always means 'go up', while it is the 'ok' gesture that means things are fine. These are much more conventional than gestures, but there are far fewer signs and much less grammar than in a full signed language. These systems are usually known as auxiliary sign systems, because of their reduced vocabulary and lack of the grammatical structures of a fully developed sign language. Not all auxiliary systems are equal in this regard: a basketball game can operate with a couple of dozen signs—essentially a context-specific set of emblem gestures—but the hand sign system developed by monastic orders could provide most necessary communication during pious periods of silence (Kendon 2004: 297–9). Auxiliary sign languages are one example of why the different phenomena in Figure 1 are arranged along a continuum; auxiliary sign systems are more complex than a series of emblems, because they have a basic grammar, but they are not as fleshed out as full independent signed languages, so they sit between the two.

Towards the signed languages end of the continuum, we also see examples of the emergence of signed communication systems from gestures. Children who are born deaf are sometimes raised in spoken language households with no signed language input. These children will often develop what is known as a 'homesign' to communicate with their family, drawing on the gestures in their home environment. These systems, used by an individual child and their caregivers, are far less ideal than ensuring children and their families can access an existing signed language, but they provide interesting insight into the insufficiency of co-speech gesture as a resource for creating language in this context. There are also examples of more developed signed systems used in households or small communities with multiple deaf people. These are occasionally known as village sign systems. The difference between a homesign system, an emerging village sign system, and a stable signed language are not absolute, and each individual context has its own unique set of circumstances. This is, again, why the continuum between gestures and signed languages is a useful way to think about various factors, rather than rigid, separate categories. Full independent signed languages are all the way to the right of the continuum in Figure 1, but there are many points along the way for alternative and auxiliary systems, as well as homesign and village sign. We return to homesign and village sign systems in Chapter 5.

For spoken languages we can make a broad distinction between speech and gestures by dividing the modalities. This division is not available when considering the boundary between gestural and grammatical features of signed languages, which is a strength of the expressive repertoire of signed languages (if perhaps a greater challenge for observing researchers). When we ask if signers gesture, Emmorey (1999: 145) suggests the answer is '[y]es, but not the way speakers do.' In signed conversation and narrative we see elements included that are not hierarchical and componential elements within the linguistic structure of the language, sometimes in use alongside signs, and sometimes in sequences of gestured actions that are not lexical signs within the language. I remember, during one session of an introductory Auslan class, we watched a video of someone narrating a story. Our teacher then asked us to list all of the signs, and their meanings, from the story. Some, like 'boy' or 'run' we had encountered already, others were new to us, like a flashing light to indicate an incoming call on a teletypewriter (TTY), or a can of drink, signed by using one hand to indicate the container and the index finger of other hand to represent pulling the tab open. When someone in the class noted the sign for *put-a-drink-on-the-table* in the story, the teacher laughed and told us that wasn't a sign, it was a gesture in the story, after introducing the can of drink. Unlike 'can', 'flash', 'TTY', and 'boy', this gesture isn't found in the Auslan Signbank. It is not a conventional sign with a stable form, but a spontaneous gesture that is only understandable in the context of that particular story; omitting or changing the gesture would not have affected the grammaticality of the narrative. The distinction between a gesture and sign in this context was opaque for learners, but easily distinguished for someone more fluent in Auslan.

In communities with high levels of bimodal bilingualism, people may integrate features of the signed language into their spoken language communication, making use of all the communicative resources available to them. In one context they are filling the role of a sign, and in another linguistic context they are functioning as co-speech gestures (albeit gestures that perhaps hold more linguistic content for conversation participants also proficient in that signed language).

The shared modality means that gestures are an important source of linguistic innovation for signed languages. It is not at all surprising that the pronominal system of many signed languages includes pointing to the self for first person, and to the interlocutor for second person. Signed languages make use of the same visual and iconic resources as co-speech gestures, because those resources are there to be used. These shared resources may be deployed differently; one corpus study of pointing in BSL and American English showed that the BSL pointing was more consistent in form, and more likely to be reduced, both features that are more typical of a linguistic system than a gestural one (Fenlon et al. 2019). It is undeniable that signed languages make use of many of the same features of iconic and contextual representation as gestures do. The important thing is to not dismiss the structural and symbolically arbitrary features of signed languages while also considering the parallels with gesture.

The shape of gesture

So far we have focused on how gesture is distinct from speech. Before we look at the integration of gesture and speech, we need to consider the structure of gestures. For all their contextual variability in form and meaning, gestures have a set of movement features in common. Understanding these features will allow us to see how they align with linguistic structures.

A gesture is a movement. It is measured from the commencement of movement until its conclusion and has a series of distinct phases. Figure 2 shows how these distinct phases combine into a gesture phrase (sometimes shortened to 'g-phrase' or 'G-phrase'). We begin with the most prominent phase, and then look at what occurs around it.

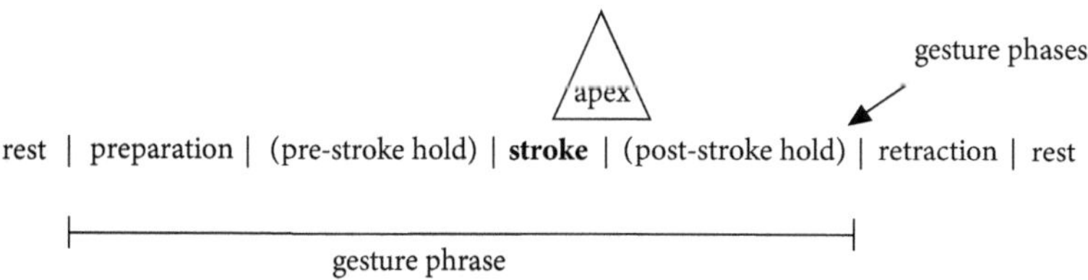

Figure 2 The structure of a gesture phrase

Stroke

The stroke is the most extended or prominent component of the gesture, and typically where the meaning of a gesture is expressed. The stroke typically aligns with any concurrent linguistic content (spoken or signed). The stroke is the full extension of an open hand while saying 'there', or the rise of the shoulders with 'know' in a shrug accompanying 'I don't know'. The stroke is the obligatory feature of the gesture, around which all the other phases occur.

Apex

The apex of the stroke is the phase when the hand or head or other part of the body is the most extended or articulated (also known as the 'peak' in some literature). It defines the time when the hand is most outstretched in a point with 'there', or the highest moment of a shoulder raise with a shrug. The degree of articulation varies considerably; a pointing gesture might involve a fully extended index finger, or it might be an almost imperceptible flick of the hand with the fingers still mostly curled, or a slight tilt of the head. The apex of a gesture can be but a fleeting moment or can be held for a considerable duration; you might hold the apex of the point you made alongside 'there' until the other person puts down the coffee they made for you. Maintenance of the apex for any length of time is entirely optional, and is known as a post-stroke hold.

Preparation

The movement leading up to the stroke of the gesture is the preparation. The preparation is a phase that begins the moment of departure from the rest position. What counts as a rest really depends on the context in which a gesture is performed; the hands may move from the lap, or from being held on the hips, or any other position, or the head may already be tilted before a gesture commences. Depending on how far the stroke of the gesture is performed from the rest position, the preparation may vary from a large movement, if the whole arm is moved from rest to far above the head to reference the giraffe you saw at the zoo yesterday, or a tiny movement, if you already have your hands on the table and use a small emphasizing gesture to stress that the zoo was very crowded. Sometimes there may be virtually no preparation at all, especially if the gesture is being performed immediately after the apex of a prior gesture, if my hands were already up high to gesture about the height of giraffes, I might also gesture about the foliage in their enclosure while my hand was up there. Alternatively, there might be a pause between the preparation and the stroke of a gesture, in an optional phase known as a pre-stroke hold. This might happen if I stretch my hand up and wait a moment before indicating the bushy foliage of the tree.

To place this all together, we move from some posture of rest, into preparation, and then the stroke, which has an apex at the maximal point of articulation and which can be optionally held. All of these phases of the gesture are considered important for the performance of a gesture and its alignment with speech and as such are the phases that constitute a gesture phrase.

Rest/recovery

Having looked at what happens before the stroke, now let's see what occurs after the stroke. There are two general options for what can happen; (1) the person may return to a rest position, a phase known as retraction or recovery, or (2) the person may use this gesture as the point of preparation for another gesture. We will look at each of these scenarios in turn.

Scenario one: the parts of the body used for the gesture can return to a rest position. This can either be the same position as prior to the performance of the gesture, or a different one. This phase is known as either the retraction or the recovery. The retraction is a phase of gesture performance, but it is not included as an element of a gesture phrase. It is omitted from the gesture phrase because it is not directly relevant to the way gestures work with speech to create meaning. We will look at this in more detail in the next section, but one of the easiest ways to demonstrate this fact is that a recovery phase is entirely optional, and a person can move immediately from the stroke of one gesture into the preparation or stroke of the next gesture. That is our second scenario.

Scenario two: It is possible, and quite common, to string multiple gestures together, moving from the stroke or hold of one gesture into the preparation or stroke of the next gesture. Someone telling a particularly evocative story might gesture almost continuously for an extended period of time without returning to a rest position. As mentioned above, there might be periods of preparation between each of these gestures, or the speaker may move directly into the stroke of the next gesture (Oprah

Winfrey enthusiastically pointing repeatedly to audience members while exclaiming 'you get a car, and you get a car, and you get a car!' is a high-energy example of the this). A speaker may also include many post-stroke holds (or not) while moving between gestures without a single return to a rest position. The period of movement with multiple gesture phrases between rests is known as a gesture unit. It is possible for a gesture unit to contain only one gesture phrase, but things become more interesting when a gesture unit contains multiple gesture phrases.

The structure of two gesture phrases into a single gesture unit is illustrated diagrammatically in Figure 3. The gesture unit is sometimes known as the 'g-unit', or 'G-unit', not to be confused with the US East Coast hip hop group of the same name from the early 2000s.

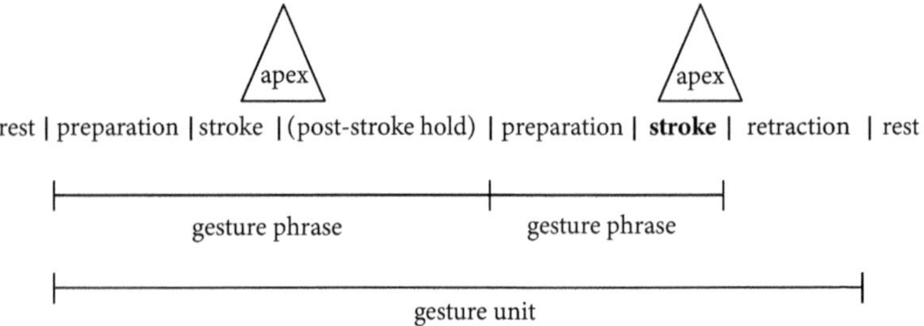

Figure 3 The structure of a gesture unit

As mentioned above, while gestures commonly demonstrate these features, the extent to which a gesture is articulated varies greatly. The stroke of a gesture could include the full extension of the arm from the shoulder, or be an almost imperceivable flick of the fingers while the hand remains at rest. Now that we know the shape of how a gesture is performed, let us consider the space in which gestures are articulated.

The space of gesture

The gesture space is usually measured with regard to how far beyond the torso a person's limbs move while they are talking. The way these movements are described draws on terminology from the field of kinesics (the study of body motion). Using this terminology can help ensure that the gestural phenomena described stand the best chance of being interpreted correctly by the reader.

The gesture space is measured with regard to the torso, because movement further away from the centre of the human body generally requires greater extension of the limbs. A common distinction is made between the centre, mid-range, and periphery of the gesture space, moving out from the centre of the torso (Figure 4), although different researchers will use different terms, or conceptualize the boundaries of the gesture space in different ways. Some researchers refer to both the mid-range and centre as 'centre' (with the tighter frame as the emphatic 'centre-centre'). Although people do not always make full use of the periphery of the gesture space, it is certainly available to them, and used when gesturing to a very far off location, or talking about trying to fetch something from a very high shelf, just out of reach. For this reason, when setting up recording equipment for gesture data collection make sure the resultant video recording will capture the full gesture space so that expansive gestures do not end up out of the camera's field.

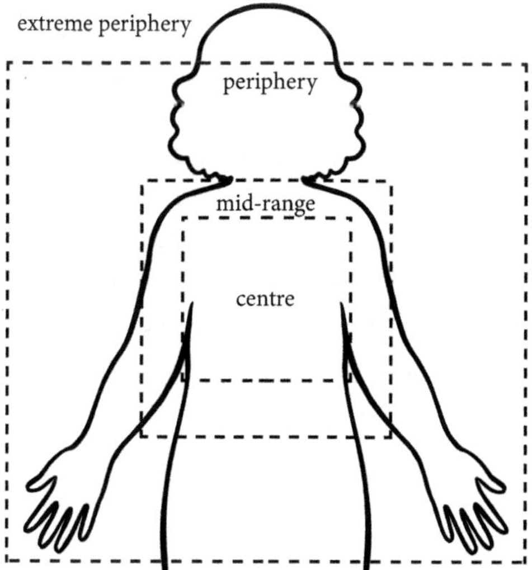

Figure 4 The gesture space
Image by Lucy Maddox

A similar distinction in location is made in the study of sign language articulation, where it is known as the 'sign space'. The sign language literature tends to provide more detail regarding distinctions in the sign space, particularly with regard to space on and around the face, as different places of articulation result in lexical differences.

With regards to gesture, some people make use of a larger gesture space than others. The degree of extension and articulation can depend on the context, the individual, or cultural variation. Some cultures tend to use a larger gesture space; work has been done showing this is the case for Italian and Spanish speakers (Efron 1941; Müller 1998), which is distinct from the frequency of gesture use across a conversation. In fact, Müller (1998) noted that Spanish speakers in her study didn't necessarily use more gestures than German speakers, they just used more of the gesture space, but this appears to be the basis for the reputation of Spanish speakers as being heavy gesture users. This is why quantifying the use of the gesture space is as important as noting frequency of gesture. There are other features of culture that can influence gesture; Kita and Essegbey (2001) noted that pointing with the left hand in Ghana tends to be restricted due to a taboo on left-hand use.

Addressees spend relatively little time looking directly at gestures. Beattie (2016) reports on a study where iconic gestures in short videos drew direct gaze only 2.1 per cent of the time, with the majority of participants' focus on the face. The lack of direct focus on gestures did not affect people's capacity to use gestural information in responding to questions about information in the videos, including information that came through the gestural channel. Other studies using gaze tracking show similar tendencies. The human eye is very good at tracking movement in the peripheral field of vision, and incorporating this information alongside speech. Gullberg and Holmqvist (2006) found that what was most likely to draw attention to a gesture was a gestural hold, as well as speakers directing their own attention to their gestures.

We've seen that the gesture space radiates from the centre, and we can talk about the different directions away from the torso that gestures can be performed (Figure 5). We can move in the vertical plane, up above the head and down below the torso, or the horizontal plane, from left to right (also known as the lateral plane). When discussing movement on the horizontal plane, the convention is to refer to left and right as they are oriented to the speaker, unless explicitly stated that you are discussing the viewpoint of an observer who has a particular orientation to the speaker. The gesture space is three dimensional, so we also need to account for the movement away, in front of, or behind, from the centre of the gesture space, which is known as the sagittal plane.

The best way to describe how people move their body in the gesture space is to describe the articulation of movement of the relevant limb(s), rather than just describing where the periphery of the limb ends up. For arms, this means describing the movement of the shoulder, elbow, wrist, and fingers. Fingers, in English, are usually referenced using their colloquial names: thumb, index, middle, ring, and pinky. For the arm to extend to the periphery of the gesture space, the articulatory

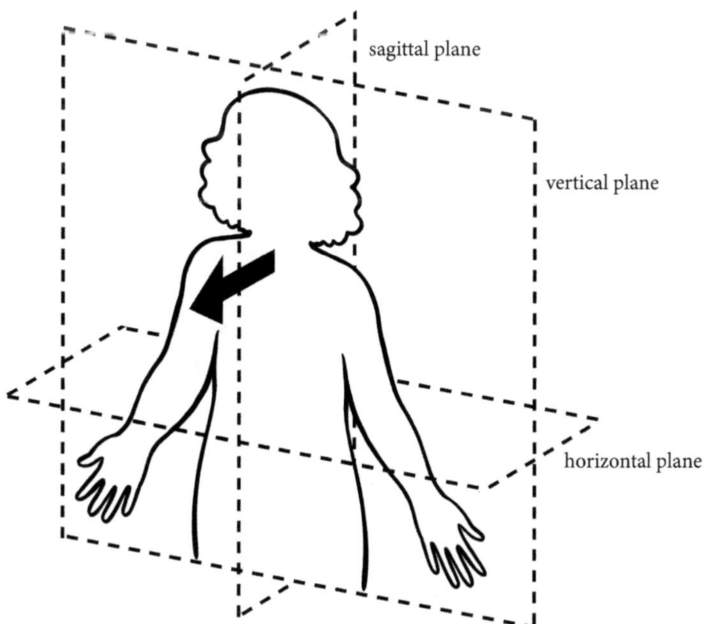

Figure 5 Planes of movement in the gesture space
Image by Lucy Maddox

movement has to happen at the shoulder. The smallest gestures are usually just an extension of a finger. Many gestural actions involve multiple points of extension; a dramatic shrug can involve a raise of the shoulders, an extension of the shoulder, a bend at the elbow, a rotation of the forearm, and a further extension at the wrist. Although I refer to limbs above, I have illustrated the movements with examples using the arm. It is also possible for the legs to also be involved in gesturing, but the majority of gesturing draws on the arms. The same principles of observation and description can be used for the legs and head (with the neck as the point of articulation) as well. Becoming more aware of the ways the body moves to perform gestures can help you see where the constraints on movement are, and why there are tendencies and preferences to perform movements in particular ways. For example, the research on pointing often notes that the thumb will be used to point behind the speaker. This is because it is often easier to bend the elbow and extend the thumb to clearly point backwards than it is to extend any of the other fingers.

The orientation of the limbs is described in terms of articulation at the joints, but also in terms of the orientation of the limbs, where rotation is possible. The hand is described as supine when the palm is facing upward, and prone when facing downwards. Physiologically, this occurs because of the pronation (rotation) of the forearm below the elbow, as the wrist does not rotate independently of the forearm.

Some subfields of gesture studies draw on particular traditions when it comes to the description of gestures. One common descriptive practice is to use the conventional handshape terminology from signed language phonology to describe the way the fingers are articulated in the performance of a gesture. Signed languages each have their own set of phonologically valid handshapes, and there has been conventionalization of their names, mostly from the equivalent ASL alphabet handshape letter or an ALS lexical item. For example, someone gesturing with all five fingers fully extended and spread out from each other might be described as using a '5 handshape', which is how this handshape is discussed in ASL phonology.

Integration of speech and gesture

Above, we saw how gestures sit alongside language and are also a part of language. Now that we have a clearer idea of some of the structural features of gestures, we can pull apart this superficial contradiction. Gestures sit alongside the linguistic structures that are often analysed as the linguistic content of language, in that the two have different structural properties. Thanks to writing, telephones, and radio, we also know that it is possible to communicate using language without invoking gestural information. While communication is possible in these contexts, it does not mean we are drawing upon the full extent of language.

Indeed, if we take a more expansive definition of language as a tool of communication, and explore the cognitive underpinnings of language, gesture is an intractable part of this human capacity. The compulsion to gesture alongside speech is so strong that even if the arms and head are restrained, a person talking will be seen moving their fingers, eyebrows, and lips at greater frequency in compensation (Rimé et al. 1984). We can also see the tight integration of speech and gesture from the fact that co-speech gestures reflexively get larger in noisy environments just as speech gets louder (known as the Lombard effect for speech), even though noise doesn't affect visual perception (Trujillo et al. 2021).

We will return to the integration of modalities regarding both the communication of meaning and the cognitive underpinnings of language processing throughout this book. For now, we will look at the temporal integration of gestures with speech. There are three features of temporal alignment for spoken languages and gesture that we will explore. The first is the alignment of the stroke of a gesture with phonological features of language. The second is the alignment of the stroke of a gesture with the semantic content of the speech. The third is the alignment of gesture with the pragmatic function of the speech. Not all of these features are as relevant, or relevant in the same way, for signed languages, because they do not involve the alignment of two different modalities that can be articulated simultaneously.

Phonological synchrony

The performance of a gesture tends to align with phonological features in the speech stream (Birdwhistell 1970; Kendon 1980; McNeill 1992), which is known as phonological alignment. There have been two related observations regarding how this occurs. The first is that the stroke of a gesture tends to align with a prominent phonological feature, such as stress in English. In this form of alignment, the apex of a gesture stroke tends to occur with, or slightly before, the phonologically prominent syllable. The second observation is that there is also another, looser, feature of alignment where the performance of a gesture phrase (from preparation to the hold of a stroke), tends to align with intonational units. For the gesture to line up with speech, this means it cannot just be spontaneous, because the body has to start moving ahead of time to meet the target; if I'm going to point while saying 'over there', I have to start moving my hands while saying 'put the flowers' so that the gesture and speech are timed together. Timing speech and gesture together means gesture is planned as part of the complex utterance and is not a decorative afterthought.

Loehr (2012) provides us with a detailed experimental investigation of the phonological alignment of gesture and speech, in a corpus of English-language conversations. Loehr annotated gesture phases, and also intonational features at three levels: pitch accents (the smallest unit), intermediate intonational units, and intonational phrases (the largest). Loehr's statistical analysis noted only two relationships, which confirmed existing observations; the apex of the gesture aligned with pitch accents, and the gesture phrase aligned with intermediate intonational phrases. The relationship between the apex of a gesture and the pitch accent in a word indicates statistical support for phonological alignment, although it is worth noting that this relationship is on a normal distribution curve, indicating there is more possibility of the stroke of the gesture occurring after the pitch accent than earlier work indicated. The relationship between intermediate intonational phrases and gesture phrases was slightly looser in Loehr's data, but around two thirds of gesture phrases aligned with this intonational unit, which is shorter than a full intonational phrase. The gesture slightly preceded the intonational unit in execution, demonstrating that, as Loehr puts it, 'gesture surfaces first, and is not a by-product of the utterance' (2012: 86).

In languages without the phonological stress systems of languages like English, the stroke will align with some other feature of prominence. In French (Rohrer et al. 2019) and Pwo Karen (Hsieh 2012) the stroke aligns with the prosodically prominent word in the utterance, although the alignment in the data from both of these languages was much less consistent than has been shown for stress-based languages such as English. This suggests that there is still a lot to finesse in our understanding of the temporal alignment of speech and gesture.

Some insight into the temporal integration of speech and gesture has come from studying the speech and gesture production of people who stutter. In a controlled experimental task, people who stutter almost never started gesturing during a stuttering disfluency. If a gesture had been started before the onset of stuttering, the gesture would be held in place until the stuttering had finished. Stuttering disrupts the flow of gestures, in a way that is not seen for other speech-simultaneous manual actions—such as pressing a button or writing the stuttered word (Mayberry and Jaques 2000). This is evidence that gesture is more integrated with language production than these other types of actions.

Phonological synchrony is so pervasive that manipulating the timing of a gesture can affect where English speakers perceive word stress (Bosker and Peeters 2021). We saw above that the stroke of a gesture in English tends to line up with a stressed syllable. Bosker and Peeters created an experimental context in which they manipulated where in a sentence a speaker would use an emphasizing gesture (we will meet these 'beat gestures' in the next chapter). By changing where in the sentence the beat gesture was performed, participants would perceive the stress in the sentence differently, imagining a stressed syllable when they saw a beat gesture. Bosker and Peeters describe this finding as a 'manual McGurk effect', drawing an analogy with how video-editing trickery of watching a mouth closing like a /g/ while a /b/ sound is played will make the viewer hear a /d/.

Semantic synchrony

In addition to temporal alignment at the phonological level, gestures also align with speech in meaning. This is known as semantic alignment. For example, a pointing gesture will align with the reference in speech to what is being pointed at (whether that is a noun—'the flower'—or a pronoun—'that'). This co-expressive feature of gesture takes many different forms, but often the gestural and linguistic components work together as an ensemble to create a more complex meaning. I often think back to a conversation I had in Nepal while trying to figure out the difference between two Yolmo words, both of which I had initially translated as 'cut'. In the conversation, it was the gestures of the woman explaining the difference to me that helped clarify the difference; *ŋá* was the sweeping horizontal action of slashing grass, while *túp* was a more general cutting word, which could be used for the vertical chopping of vegetables or firewood.

The global and synthetic features of gestures allow them to work in combination with speech, particularly in depicting visual and spatial information that requires the context of the speech stream to be understood. We have two forms of evidence that the semantic integration of gesture and speech is an important feature of communication. The first is that a person who is asked to repeat something they have just said will typically repeat both the spoken and gestural content, indicating that both are considered important for clear communication. The second is that a person who retells a story they have seen someone tell will include information from both the spoken and gestural elements of the story (McNeill et al. 1994). If I were telling a story about finding my keys after I thought I had lost them, and gesture the action of pulling them out of a pocket, someone might retell the story noting that I found them in the pocket of the skirt I was wearing, based on the gestural information.

Pragmatic synchrony

We can also look at the pragmatic alignment of speech and gesture. This is where the speech and gesture align in their function within the discourse, rather than with regard to the content of the discourse. Loehr (2012) noted that intonation units that finish on a downward pitch to convey the completion of the utterance will often be accompanied by gestures that return to the rest position, which also indicates the speaker's turn is done. An intonation pitch that marks incompleteness can be accompanied by a shrug, or a hand that is raised in a hold to indicate the speaker plans to continue gesturing, and therefore speaking. Gesture is an important resource in negotiating turn-taking in conversation, with incomplete gestures signalling that a turn is not concluded (Kendrick et al. 2023).

The fact that we see phonological, semantic, and pragmatic alignment in language and gesture may initially seem to be unremarkable, but the cognitive implications of this feat are worth considering. For the stroke of a gesture to be executed at the same time as the relevant words, the preparation for the gesture must commence beforehand; in order for our hand to be outstretched at the apex of a pointing gesture at the same time as we say 'over there', the preparation has to commence well in advance. Indeed, researchers note that gesture tends to actually occur slightly before the parallel speech (Schegloff 1984: 291; ter Bekke et al. 2020), not after, which means gesture is, indeed, central to the planning of the full utterance, and not an afterthought. Gesture and speech have to be pre-planned in coordination so that they can be executed simultaneously. The important lesson that speech and gesture alignment have for us is that gesture is more than ornamental, and it is in the combination of speech and gesture that the full extent of linguistic meaning is expressed. We will look more closely at the cognitive relationship between speech and gesture in Chapter 6.

How we study gesture

Gesture Studies draws on different research methods from a range of disciplines. Each of these approaches has their merits, and this book draws on research that takes many different approaches to understanding gesture. Most gesture research is focused on the production of gesture, but there is also research on the way people pay attention to gesture as well. While there are a diversity of research methods in Gesture Studies, there is still plenty of capacity to expand the range of languages and contexts in which gesture is studied. For example, in a survey of emblems that I conducted with Kensy Cooperrider, we found that the majority of research focused on languages of Europe and select regions of Africa, Central and South America, and Japan (Gawne and Cooperrider 2024). There is much scope for work to be done to understand the world's gestural diversity.

Observational methods allow us the opportunity to understand the full richness of what people can do with gesture, in a variety of social contexts. Observational studies might provide a detailed analysis of the use of gesture in a single interaction, or might look at the recurring use of gesture across a number of interactions, in different contexts, or with different participants. Observational data require the researcher to be very familiar with the conversational context in order to draw a rich interpretation of what is being depicted in the gestural channel. This often means recordings are conducted in people's daily environment, or are made with groups of people who are comfortable and familiar with talking to each other. Haviland (2000) has spent years working with, and videoing, the stories of Zinacantec Tzotzil speakers in Mexico and Guugu Yimithirr speakers in Australia, looking at the way they use language, including gesture, and how this is tied to language, culture, and context. We will return to Haviland's work with Guugu Yimithirr story-tellers in Chapter 4. We also now have an abundance of video of all kinds of genres of language use that can be used to answer questions about gesture; Cirillo (2019) used an existing corpus of academic presentations to study the use of 'air quote' gestures in English, showing how speakers used this gesture to distance themselves from the content of the spoken channel.

In contrast to observational studies, experimental design constrains the context of communication so that researchers can track or manipulate the variables involved. One of the most commonly used experimental designs in Gesture Studies is to have study participants consume a piece of media and then retell the story or describe the stimulus content. In doing this, researchers can better interpret the gestures in the context of the stimulus, and also compare the gestures used by multiple participants who are all working from the same original input. Media in these studies are usually printed cartoon stories or short animations or performances. While some videos are created by the research teams to control the stimulus, existing cartoons are also popular. In particular, the 1949

Warner Bros. cartoon 'Canary Row' about Sylvester the cat attempting to catch Tweety the canary features in numerous studies, for the excellent range of motion events during the fast-paced hijinks. In this guide we will see work from McNeill (1992), Kita and Özyürek (2003), and Emmorey et al. (2008a) that all make use of this cartoon. When retelling a story, participants will often have someone in the room to listen to their story. This is frequently another participant in the experiment who is hearing the story for the first time and creates a naturalistic context of responses. Sometimes it will be a confederate of the experiment team, either to subvert their role as audience or to provide a consistent set of responses across all participants.

A common methodological thread across all gesture research is the importance of affordable video recording as it became more widely available in the mid-twentieth century, and digital video transcription and analysis software that has subsequently become available in the twenty-first century. The ability to capture interaction in a variety of contexts in a relatively unobtrusive way has allowed for the emergence of fine-grained analysis of the relationship between speech and gesture, and comparison of gesture use across interactions. For this kind of work, we need to make sure participants are gesturing and speaking in a way that is comfortable and natural for them (unless we are intentionally manipulating the context!). Covert video recording will not pass muster with ethics review boards, but people are often not monitoring their gesturing even in recorded situations, so the gestures people use in most data collection methods are considered indicative of general usage. When people's gestures are called to their attention, they can become self-conscious about the way they gesture. It is partly for this reason that you will find that many gesture research labs will typically have names like the 'Communication Development Lab' at Warwick University or the 'Multimodal Language Department' at the Max Planck Institute for Psycholinguistics. In this way, participants are not primed to self-consciousness by lab signage or consent forms.

Although it has become easier to record gesture-use, transcribing those gestures is still a time-consuming and highly-skilled job. Over the last two decades the research standard for transcription software has been ELAN (currently Version 6.8, 2024). In ELAN, annotations can be aligned to video and audio. You can link and embed annotations, and annotate different features on different tiers of the annotation. Figure 6 is a screenshot of an ELAN transcription for a recording of Larkel, a Syuba speaker, from an analysis of the type of rotated palm gesture he is performing in the video still (Gawne 2018: 20). You can see the video recording in the top left quadrant, and the waveform of the sound running along the middle. There are tiers for the Syuba language transcription (in a Devanagari orthography), and for the Nepali and English translations. There are then tiers that segment each gesture phrase and also the phases within each. The interface allows the user to move across the timeline, moving the video, audio, and transcriptions.

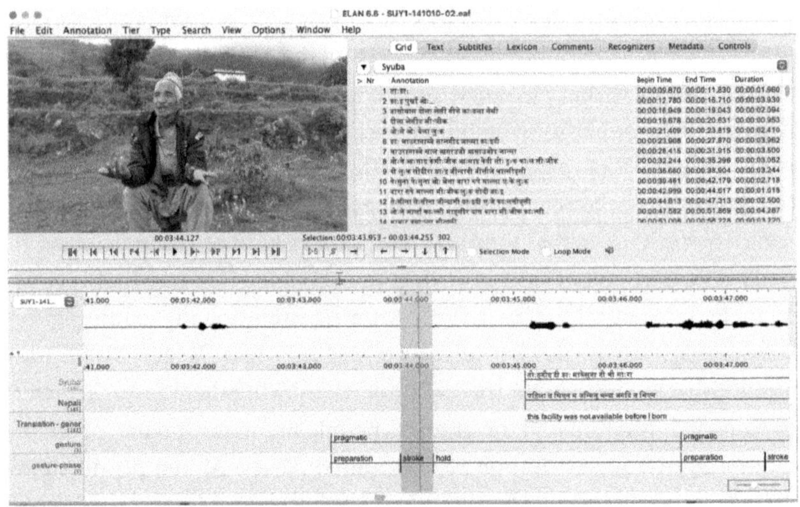

Figure 6 Screenshot of an ELAN annotation file

Gesture research will usually include some discussion of intercoder reliability in selecting gestures or ascribing categories to them. This involves more than one person, trained in the coding protocol, coding at least a portion of the data with results then being compared. Even studies with clear methods and processes may only achieve 90 per cent intercoder reliability (Kita et al. 1998), given the complexity of transcribing gestural data. Researchers are experimenting with automated transcription of gesture, and motion capture techniques (e.g. Trujillo et al. 2019) that will undoubtedly make the data analysis process easier, allowing for larger scale studies and new, quantifiable insights.

Key milestones in gesture studies

The International Society for Gesture Studies was founded in 2002. This was not a sudden materialization of an interest in gesture, but the formalization of a network of scholars who had been working on topics within gesture in the late twentieth century (Müller 2002). While there are certainly some uses of the term 'gesturology', these are mostly a playful acknowledgement that while gesture is a topic worthy of study, the formalization of the research agenda in this area is very much a modern one.

The outline in this section is not a history of Gesture Studies, as there has never been a single scholarly lineage. These are just some of the times when gesture has captured people's attention before the emergence of Gesture Studies as a dedicated field, and key works that are often referenced in the gesture literature. Kendon (2004) provides a great deal more detail about the history of the study of gesture.

The earliest recorded Western literature to engage with gesture was within the Greek and Roman tradition of oration. Gesture was one rhetorical device that a speaker had at their disposal to make their argument more compelling, and it thus received attention in the literature on oratory. Aristotle, in *Rhetoric* (fourth century BCE), was less interested in gesture and other rhetorical performance skills such as use of voice, and more interested in the crafting of compelling arguments using facts. This view was not shared by everyone in the Classical world. The *Institutio oratoria* (Institutes of Oratory) was written by Marcus Fabius Quintilianus, known as Quintilian, and published sometime in the late first century CE. In this twelve-volume work, Quintilian outlines fundamentals of oratory, providing us with the most complete surviving work on this topic. In Book XI (Section III) Quintilian explains that, in the delivery of oratory, the speaker needs to consider both voice and movement, and understands the value of gesture in conveying meaning in persuasive speaking. Like any good public speaking advisor, he goes on to describe the most elegant handshapes, most compelling speed and trajectory of moment, and most meaningful actions, and also discusses what not to do (including the misstep of exposing your side if you stretch too far in your toga while gesturing). In this tradition the use of gesture is based on considered, conscious training. Quintilian notes 'we cannot hope to obtain perfection unless nature is assisted by study' (XI, III, 11). This discussion of oratory training is quite different to our contemporary focus on more spontaneous communication, however Quintilian's work is important as one of the most vibrant discussions of ephemeral multimodal communication from this period.

Gesture returns as a topic of interest in the Renaissance, partly thanks to a rediscovery of the full original texts of authors such as Aristotle, Cicero, and Quintilian. This led to new work that considered the role of gesture in communication. In 1616 Giovanni Bonifacio, of Vicenza in northeast Italy, published *L'Arte de 'Cenni*, which is a detailed account of the communicative intent of a variety of gestures, postures, and clothing. Similarly, in London in 1644, John Bulwar wrote two volumes on gesture: the *Chirologica*, which looked at 'natural' gestures, and *Chironomia*, which instructed the reader on elevating gesture through the study of oratory. Alongside an interest in the rhetorical and artistic merit of gesture, there was a growing interest in the signed communication of deaf people. Abbé Charles-Michel de l'Epée was the first to effectively develop a method for instructing deaf students using a signed form of French. Bringing deaf people, and their existing repertoires, together from across the country created a context for this new French Sign Language (LSF) to thrive. l'Epée's successor took French sign to the USA, which was one key element in the development of what is ASL (American Sign Language) today. In parallel developments in the UK, BSL (British Sign Language) emerged out of local signed languages, as schools for the deaf were developed.

Edward Tylor (1865/1964), William Wundt (1900/2010), and Garrick Mallery (1881/1972) all examined the role of gesture in human expression and the evolution of language. Mallery's work also included documentation of the Plains Indian Sign Language, used across central Canada, the central and western United States of America, and northern Mexico. Charles Darwin also saw value in gesture as a way of studying evolution. In 1872 he published *The Expression of the Emotions in Man and Animals*, and speculated on the evolutionary origins of gestures such as the nod and shrug. Darwin also considered other features of communication such as facial expressions, drawing on observations of different animals, as well as cross-cultural observations of humans. A key work from the nineteenth century in a very different genre was Andrea de Jorio's meticulously observed study of the use of gesture in Naples (Jorio 1832/2000 is a fantastic translation into English from Kendon).

Although there was some good work at this time, it was not entirely a period with positive ramifications for the long-term vitality of the discipline. At the Second International Congress on Education of the Deaf in Milan in 1880, the participants passed a motion banning signed modality education in deaf schools, and requiring schools to offer exclusively spoken education. This move was a devastating imposition on the rights of deaf students, and even though we now know of the importance of signed language in deaf education, oralism still hinders many students' access to education and community today. The de-prioritization of signed languages also greatly hindered research on their linguistic structure and contributed to the devaluation of the visual modality both in communication and in research.

In parallel to this very Western story of gesture, there are other traditions with a focus on the manual modality. One example is the Mudras of Hindu, Buddhist, and Jain ritual. These configurations of the body, and most often the hands, are part of both the spiritual practice and iconography of these religions, including in meditation and art (Saunders 1985). *Mudra* is the Sanskrit name for these handshapes, and means 'seal' or 'gesture' but a similar set of handshapes are found across religions and languages in the region, often with names that carry similar meanings. One example is the *abhayamudra* the 'gesture of fearlessness'. This gesture involves the right hand being held with the palm upwards and outwards, with the fingers held together and extended upward too. The gesture is one of benevolence, peace, and protection, intended to dispel fear. It is used in representations of Hindu gods including Parvati and the Nataraja depiction of Shiva. In Buddhism, there is a documented story that the Buddha used this gesture to calm a drunk elephant that attacked him (Ekottarāgama 18.5). Learning the Mudras allows you to read the lessons in religious sculptures, paintings, and other artworks. A number of Mudras are also incorporated into the practice of some yoga traditions, and of Indian traditional dance. Sometimes these have a connection to the religious Mudras, but there are approximately fifty Mudras in Indian dance, and they have developed into a specific lexicon that is part of the narrative of traditional dance. For example, the *chandrakala*, is made with the index finger and thumb extended into an L, and this handshape is used to represent the moon, while the *hamsasya* 'swan beak' is made with the thumb and index pinched, and the other fingers extended, and can be used to represent many things including tying thread and drawing. There are other regional traditions of the use of gesture for ritual or oratory effect, as well as the emergence of local sign languages, alternate sign language, and auxiliary sign systems which have their own artistic traditions.

In the twentieth century the ability to record high-fidelity video at an affordable price finally allowed research to overcome the ephemerality of gesture. David Efron and Ray Birdwhistell were two anthropologists who saw the value of applying this technology to capturing and analysing gesture. Efron's (1941/1972) study of the use of gesture by Italian and Eastern European Jewish migrants to the USA included video recordings of conversation. This allowed Efron to quantify the number of gestures used, and analyse the physical gesture space each speaker employed. In looking at migrants from these two communities, and their first-generation American children, Efron showed that there were differences in the way Italians and Eastern European Jews gestured, but these differences were less marked, or absent, in the next generation. This demonstrated that gestures are culturally learnt, a direct challenge to Nazi theory at the time that difference in gesture is a result of racial inheritance. Unfortunately, we do not know what became of Efron's original recordings, all we have left are the wonderfully dynamic illustrations by Stuyvesant Van Veen in the published volume.

Birdwhistell (1970) championed video's role in meticulous analysis, and founded the field of kinesics, which looks at the broader field of communicative body motions of which gesture is one component. Birdwhistell made extensive use of recorded data, but he approached the methodology he developed with a critical and thoughtful eye. While many of the limitations of film that Birdwhistell discussed are no longer obstacles, such as difficulty in data replay, he does note that there are a number of potential pitfalls in the use of video, including the problematic potential that researchers will overgeneralize observations in a specific recording to a population; '[f]rom the outset these tools have their limitations and these limitations must be recognised or the shapes they record or transmit can become so real as to obscure the very nature they were designed to abstract' (Birdwhistell 1970: 152).

In 1956 Ruesch and Kees coined the term 'nonverbal communication' (NVC) in their book of the same name. Their interest expanded beyond gesture to also include gaze and posture, as well as clothing and environmental objects. The work of Efron, Birdwhistell, and Ruesch and Kees set the stage for an increased interest in gesture in the second half of the twentieth century. Some of this included the proliferation of literature on 'body language', which departs from earlier NVC work and contemporary Gesture Studies in that it seeks to give consistent meaning to communicative actions that are largely dependent on the specific interactional context. Gesture will not always reveal people's lies and hidden opinions, but it does have the capacity to give us a richer understanding of the cognitive and cultural underpinnings of human communication. The history of Gesture Studies is only the beginning. Throughout the rest of this guide we will see where contemporary research has taken this field of study.

Conclusion

In this chapter we have looked at the nature of gesture, and how it relates to spoken and signed language. Gesture co-occurs with spoken and signed languages, which is possible because gesture and language have different properties. Gesture and signed languages share a modality, but they are so different in their structure that gesture is used with signed languages. Language has structure that is hierarchical and combinatoric with standards of form that allow it to be context-independent. Gesture is global and non-combinatoric in how it creates meaning. The lack of standards of form mean that it is context-dependent for its meaning. We can see evidence for the integration of gesture and language by looking at the alignment of gesture with phonological, semantic, and pragmatic features of language.

There are some common features to the performance of gesture. A gesture phrase commences when we move from rest. The structure of a gesture has phases including the preparation, optional pre-stroke hold, a stroke with an apex at the maximal point of articulation, and then an optional post-stroke hold. From there it is possible to have a retraction and return to rest, or commence another gesture phrase, which builds multiple gesture phrases into a gesture unit. The gesture space includes close, mid-range, and peripheral zones expanding away from the torso along the vertical, horizontal, and sagittal planes.

Different observational and experimental methods in Gesture Studies research have all benefited from advances in video recording and digital transcription technology. Gesture has been a topic of interest across recorded history, from the oratory of ancient Greece and Rome, to the Mudras of Hinduism and Buddhism, and the Enlightenment interest in the origins of human language. The formalized understanding of gesture is the result of sustained interest in gesture in the second half of the twentieth century.

Further reading and resources

For more detail on every topic covered in this Slim Guide, and many, many more besides, we are very fortunate to have the majestic two volumes of *Body—Language—Communication: An International Handbook on Multimodality in Human Interaction* (Müller et al. 2013, 2014). These two volumes include 171 short chapters, which feature a wide range of disciplinary perspectives, methods, and languages. The more recent, and more compact, *Cambridge Handbook of Gesture Studies* (Cienki 2024) includes 26 chapters on both theory and methodology.

For a general introduction to why Gesture Studies is such an interesting topic of study, Lingthusiasm Episode 30 *Why do we gesture when we speak?* is 34 minutes long and available in audio and video formats (transcript also available).[1]

---

[1] https://lingthusiasm.com/post/183,615,937,296/lingthusiasm-episode-30-why-do-we-gesture-when-we

3

Gesture categorization

In the previous chapter, we looked at how co-speech gestures contrast with other kinds of bodily actions. This chapter provides an overview of major co-speech gesture categories identified in the Gesture Studies literature, including their features and implications for our understanding of human communication. Before we look at these categories, we start with an overview of the history and general structure of gesture categorization. We then look at five major gesture categories; iconic, metaphoric, pointing, beat, and recurrent. We also revisit emblems, which were introduced in Chapter 2. After introducing these common categories we return to a discussion of the complexities of applying a category approach to gesture.

Some notes on terminology at the top of this chapter: co-speech gestures are sometimes called 'gesticulations' in the gesture continuum outlined in Chapter 2. Gesticulation is a useful term when contrasting co-speech gestures with other gestural phenomena such as emblems. In this chapter, we use the more common term 'gesture'.

Why categories of gesture?

This chapter is intended to help you navigate common categories in the Gesture Studies literature, and is not a definitive set of categories or a definitive way that all researchers approach gesture categorization. There are several things to consider when approaching gestural categories. The first is to understand what questions you are trying to answer in your own research. The second is to understand the formal and functional

Gesture. Lauren Gawne, Oxford University Press. © Lauren Gawne (2025).
DOI: 10.1093/9780198951377.003.0003

properties of categories and how these relate to your question. The final thing to consider is which definition of a category you are using, and to be clear about this in your own research design, execution, and writing.

Different co-speech gestures have different functions, and gestures with the same function can also show similar formal properties. Therefore, gesture categorization draws on both functional and formal properties of a gesture. Gesture categorization requires attention to the context in which a gesture is performed; the same handshape in different contexts can be used for gestures that have different functions. For example, you may think of an extended index finger as a prototypical pointing gesture (in the deictic category), but the same extended finger might, in another context, be an iconic gesture illustrating a moment in a story about someone pressing a button in an elevator. Assigning a gesture to a particular category always requires this communicative context.

Even the earliest literature on gesture observed that co-speech gestures have a variety of functions; Quintilian discussed pointing and mimicry as well as a variety of gesticulations used for persuasion and emphasis, and de Jorio listed the gestures he observed, alphabetically by function (including, but not limited to *amore* 'love', *danaro* 'money', and *offriere* 'offering') (Jorio 1832/2000). Efron (1941/1972) noted a variety of communicative functions of the gestures he was observing, although his interests were more in the nature of how these gestures were performed. Ekman and Friesen (1969) used Efron's work as the basis for a more systematic approach to the categories that emerged from his data, and their own work (Ekman and Friesen 1972). Ekman further entrenched this approach in his extended introduction to the 1972 reprint of Efron's work. This categorization was influential in McNeill's (1992) presentation of gesture categories, which is a highly influential source, and often cited as the basis of category definitions by other researchers (Skubisz 2017).

We will now explore six major gesture categories. For each category there is a basic definition, and a summary list of other labels these categories have been given in the research literature. There are examples of these gestures to help illustrate the formal and functional features of each category. Finally, we explore one area of the research literature that has used this gesture category to explore a question in human communication. These are not the only uses to which these categories have been put; we will continue to encounter each of these categories of gesture in the subsequent chapters of this book.

Iconic gestures

Iconic gestures depict the physical properties of things in the world.

Some prototypical examples: indicating the size of a fish, depicting how quickly a plane flew by, demonstrating how fluffy a cat is.

Names for this category: iconic (McNeill 1992), depictive (Wundt 1900/2010), physiographic (Efron 1941/1972), pictographic and kinetographic (Ekman and Friesen 1969).

Iconic gestures can be used to represent features of objects, or actions undertaken. Iconic gestures relate specifically to physical objects and actions. The abstract domain is represented by metaphoric gestures, discussed below, although they certainly share similar properties of form. There was a brief fashion for referring to iconic gestures as iconix in the plural (e.g. McNeill and Levy 1982), which did not last, but looked very cool.

Iconic gestures can relate to what they are representing in a number of ways. An iconic gesture might model some element of an object being referred to, or depict the object as though sculpting or sketching the shape of it. Modelling would be using the fingers to represent the spines on a pufferfish, while depiction would be tracing the outline of an inflated spherical spiny pufferfish. An iconic gesture might also be an enactment, such as if you were to puff out your own arms and cheeks to do an impression of a pufferfish reacting to a threat.

Iconic gestures can relate to different viewpoints on an action. They might represent an observer's viewpoint; in a story about a car race the narrator's hands might represent two cars and their hair-raisingly close positions. Iconic gestures can also take on the perspective of a character in the narrative, perhaps one of the drivers with their hands on the wheel taking quick glances at their encroaching competitor. There's no obligation for the narrator to have been the character to take on this gestural viewpoint; a compelling storyteller might move between viewpoints throughout the narrative to enrich the story.

Iconic gestures are influenced by the physical properties of what they are representing. McNeill (1992: 221–2 see also McNeill and Duncan 2000) noted iconic gesture commonalities across language groups as people described the same Sylvester and Tweety cartoon. Events such as a bowling ball being dropped down a drainpipe were enacted in similar ways, with the direction of the action reflecting the action they had seen. The representation of witnessed events and entities leads to these commonalities, but this does not mean that iconic gestures exist in some state of unfiltered iconic representation. Although the representation of the physical world is the impetus for iconic gestures, this category of gestures is not free of the influence of language. Kita and Özyürek (2003) demonstrated that the structural properties of verbs can affect the performance of iconic gestures across languages. We will return to this work in detail in Chapter 4.

Metaphoric gestures

Metaphoric gestures depict abstract concepts as having physical properties.

> **Some prototypical examples**: moving the hand upward to show improvement, indicating ahead to refer to tomorrow, placing two arguments on the left and right of your gesture space.

> **Names for this category**: metaphoric (McNeill 1992; Parrill 2008).

Culturally constructed metaphors provide us with a shared basis to discuss abstract concepts using concrete properties. Temperature takes on a spatial feature of height when we talk about the temperature 'going up' as it gets hotter. Virtue also takes on a spatial property with 'good' things relating to 'up' and 'bad' things 'down' (from 'feeling down', to a 'pick me up' coffee, to the geography of heaven and hell). Even the way that we talk about ideas being small, bounded objects (often the size of an apple, snug in the palm) that can be passed around, is a metaphoric understanding of an abstract concept.

The notion of metaphoric gestures draws on the cognitive linguistic approach to metaphor, which examines metaphors that are often deeply embedded in the way that we approach abstract concepts. We use these conceptual metaphors in ways that have implications for our interpretation of events (Lakoff and Johnson 1980). In this work, researchers seek to describe the source of the metaphor and how it is systematically applied to a new, often abstract, target domain. For Western conceptions of time, that would be the source of the physical space as represented by (a) our body or (b) our writing system applied to the target domain of time. This is how we think about time with (a) the future in front of us as we move through space from the past to the future or (b) with the past to the left and time moving to the right. Often the metaphors that we use are so pervasive that we do not even realize that we are applying physical properties to the abstract domain. The pervasiveness of these metaphors is evident in how they show up across both our speech and our gesture. The pervasiveness does not mean these metaphors are universal, in Chapter 4 we will see how different cultures think, speak, and gesture about time differently.

Cienki (2008) provides an analysis of the different ways metaphor may show up in human language. First, a metaphor may show up in both the speech and the gesture. Secondly, there might be different metaphors in speech and gesture. Cienki (2008: 14–15) gives an example where the speaker is talking about moral choices as having the physical properties of bounded entities. The person says that rather than being a gradient, the choices are 'black and white', and at the same time moves their open hand between the left and right of the gesture space. In the speech, the metaphor is one of colour, in the gestures the metaphor is spatial. Together they work to build a more complex metaphor where the two choices have both spatial and colour attributes that attest to their distinctness. Thirdly, there may be no metaphor in speech, but one shows up in the gestural channel. This is what happens when we use our left-to-right time metaphor. We do not have a convention of using this metaphor in our spoken language the way that we do with the 'future ahead of us' metaphor. Even though there is no ready language for this metaphor, once you start looking for it, you see it everywhere in gestures as well as other visual contexts. That metaphoric gestures show up in the absence of language demonstrates the extent to which these metaphors are pervasive in how we approach our understanding of abstract domains.

Some researchers include metaphoric gestures with iconic gestures in their categorization. This recognizes the similarity of these two categories in terms of the way they depict and illustrate; the fact that you are holding an apple or an idea is less important than the representation of that holding action. This is particularly the case in categorization schemas dating from before the rise of work on conceptual metaphors made this topic more salient to researchers. I believe there is merit in keeping the categories distinct, as conceptual metaphors can vary across cultures in ways that can affect gesture production, and gesture provides a unique view into how people use and process these metaphors.

Metaphor can serve as a motivation for other gesture categories too. Thumbs up and thumbs down perhaps emerged, and have remained so compelling as emblems, because of their positive and negative attributes from our cultural understanding of upward being good. Their cultural salience and required standards of form mean that they are now categorically emblems (introduced below), but we can see metaphoric origins. We can also use gestures from other categories in metaphoric space. For example, we can point towards the future, a type of imagery that is often used for statues of revolutionary leaders, who continue to point towards the bright future even when the revolution is long past (Cienki and Müller 2008).

Deictic gestures

Deictic gestures indicate a place or object.

> **Some prototypical examples**: pointing at a door in the room, pointing towards the direction of the city, indicating with your head where someone was sitting at their desk yesterday.

> **Names for this category**: deictic (Efron 1941; Ekman and Friesen 1969; McNeill 1992), pointing (Kita 2003).

Deictic is the Latinized form of the Greek work *deiktikos*, which means 'able to show'. The use of the term deictic in Gesture Studies is in the linguistic tradition, rather than the philosophical one. In philosophy if an argument is deictic it involves reasoning which proves something directly (in contrast to *elenctic*, or reasoning with an indirect proof). In linguistics, deictic language is that which has a fixed sense, but what it denotes changes depending on context. For example, 'tomorrow' always means the day after today, but whether that is 21 February, or 15 December or any other date depends on what today's date is. Similarly, the pronoun 'I' changes referent depending on who is saying it.

Deictic gestures involve a characteristic movement pattern in which a body part is moved to a location in space with the intent of directing attention. The people whose attention you are seeking know not to look just at the limb that is being pointed with, but to attend to the object or location in line with the performed point. Just as the word 'tomorrow' means something different depending on the day, the same deictic gesture can refer to different things depending on where it is being directed.

It is hard to overstate just what an impressive cognitive feat it is to attend to, and understand, pointing gestures. Pointing typically emerges before words (Liszkowski et al. 2012), and is communicatively meaningful across all cultures. Almost every attempt to categorize gesture has included a category of pointing or deixis. It is this ubiquity that allows it to be an important resource for a range of communicative contexts including homesign (Goldin-Meadow et al. 1984: 113), intercultural contact situations (Hewes 1974), and for individuals with acquired language impairments such as aphasia (Goodwin 2003), and it is commonly adopted as as a way of making pronouns in signed languages (Marschark 1994). Deictic gesturing is ubiquitously human, in that it appears that our closest primate relatives do not use deictic gesturing among themselves, but can be trained to do so for humans (Tomasello 2006). Other animals have the capacity to understand pointing; domesticated dogs appear to have successfully learnt this skill after millennia of cohabitation with humans (MacLean et al. 2014).

We point, but what do we point at? We can point to objects, people, locations, and other things that participants in the conversation can see. If we were out for a walk in the park you might point out a particularly excellent tree or interesting bird. We can also point to these things even when they are not visible to the speaker or addressee. While we are in the park you might point past the horizon to where there is some grassland, or perhaps even in the direction of a country you are planning on travelling to for bird watching. How closely your deictic reference aligns with the not-visible target will vary depending on the context, but it can also vary depending on the language you speak; users of languages with absolute spatial reference (use of 'north' and 'south' instead of relative terms like 'left' and 'right') are far better at attending to absolute spatial relations and tend to do better at maintaining locational references (Levinson 1997). We can also point to abstract ideas as though they were physical objects. We might start developing a plan for our next visit to the park, and while a plan is an abstract concept, we might set it up as an imaginary physical entity on the table in front of us used to map different stages lined up in sequence (see the section 'Metaphoric gestures' above) and refer back to it with a deictic gesture throughout the conversation. And finally, we can also point to things in narrative space. If you were telling someone about our walk in the park and the excellent tree we saw, the tree might be positioned in the left of your gesturing space, allowing you to point at the tree in this location multiple times throughout the story. We can also maintain space for abstract objects in narrative space. If we were discussing two different arguments for why there should be more government funding for parks, we might set these up on the left and right of our gestural space and point back to these locations as we build our arguments.

You might think of a prototypical pointing gesture as involving an arm outstretched, with palm down and index finger prominently extended. This is certainly one type of deictic gesture, but not the only way we can do deixis. Across cultures we see common use of lip pointing (Enfield 2001) and a range of other pointing handshapes, including open hand, and middle finger pointing (Wilkins 2003). Even for English speakers, we can use our heads, eyes, and legs to point, in the right context. The multitude of different forms are why I prefer to use the category term 'deictic' rather than 'pointing', so that we consider more than just the typical pointing gestures that might come to mind for us. Some have suggested that index finger pointing is a universal human characteristic (Povinelli and Davis 1994: 134), however a range of cross-cultural gesture research has challenged this assumption (overview in Cooperrider et al. 2018b).

Beyond variation at the cultural level, we also see variation in deictic gesture use by individuals in conversation. Both Wilkins (2003) for Arrernte and Kendon (2004) for Italian and English note that an open hand point is more likely to be used for deictic reference to more than one item, such as pointing at a cluster of trees. Other variation observed by Kendon (2004) includes the use of the thumb for ease of pointing behind the speaker, especially if a specific location is not important, and the use of a palm-up open hand if the speaker wishes their audience to inspect the referred target. We can also consider examples of how we might point with our head or our foot if our hands are otherwise occupied, the pointing gesture being influenced by the specific communicative moment.

Beat gestures

Beat gestures are those with a repetitive action used for emphasis.

Some prototypical examples: the 'don't you do that!' scold with the extended wagging index finger, the gestures used by politicians to emphasize a point.

Names: baton (Efron 1941/1972; Ekman and Friesen 1969), motor movements/gestures (Hadar 1989; Krauss et al. 2000), beat (McNeill 1992).

The category of beat gestures is primarily defined by the distinct repetition of the stroke of the gesture. The way that beat gestures appear to be keeping the rhythm of the speech is how they get their name, Efron's term 'baton' similarly references this formal feature, which is a hallmark of this category. Through this repetition, the associated spoken content is given greater emphasis. It is possible that repetition can be used for other gesture categories; if you use your hand to indicate movements of a pogo stick, or shake your head in an emblematic gesture of negation, there is repetition, and greater duration can give a more emphatic interpretation, however a beat gesture emphasizes the prominence of the co-produced speech within the discourse structure. Iconic, metaphoric, and deictic gestures relate to the semantic propositional content. Beat gestures and recurrent gestures (see the next section) relate to the pragmatic effect of the propositional content.

A beat gesture aligns with the phonological rhythms of speech. In English and other languages with stress patterns, this means that the downward stroke of a beat gesture will align with the stressed sylla-ble in speech. The synchrony is not absolute; you will occasionally see someone continue a beat over a pause or note the synchrony become weaker, but broadly this synchrony is notable. The emphatic nature of beat gestures means that they can provide a way of assessing the speaker's conception of what should be attended to in the discourse structure.

This repetition is considered to be a single gesture phrase with a sin-gle, complex stroke. McNeill (1992: 321) refers to the repetition of a beat gesture as a 'biphasic' stroke. Regardless of how many times the biphasic stroke returns to the apex, the gesture is considered a single phrase from the preparation through to the end of the stroke. As with all categories of gesture, although we see the potential for extensive repetition and the complex biphasic stroke, beat gestures can also be small and underspeci-fied as with any other category. Sometimes a beat will just be a small flick of the fingers at the periphery of the gesture space. It is not uncommon to see a beat performed without preparation or recovery, instead the beat will simply commence wherever the limbs are at that moment.

Beat gestures made with the hands might come immediately to mind, particularly if we are thinking about the kinds of formal oratory that makes extensive use of beat gestures to drive home the message. The focus of categorizing beat gestures is the rhythmic repetition of the stroke, so the handshape used can vary between different beat ges-tures. The handshape may convey other information; for example, the handshape might be a pointing gesture, so the repetition of the beat emphasizes the importance of the direction. In fact, because it is this repetition of the stroke that is important, the category of beat combines well with all of the other categories. Sometimes beat gestures might even encode semantic information that we do not immediately notice. In a study of narrative retellings by eighty English speakers, Yap et al. (2018) demonstrated that speakers will encode literal or metaphoric spatial language in the subtle direction of the movement of a beat gesture. In three-quarters of the re-tellings, speakers included spatial information even if the common metaphoric language was not in the original story (e.g. 'the temperature got hotter' corresponds with an upward spatial trajectory in the beat gesture). This study is a nice cautionary reminder that beats may be conveying additional information beyond emphasis, through the speaker's choice of handshape or trajectory.

Other limbs can also be used to perform beat gestures. A nod of the head has the additional semantic benefit of conveying agreement on top of emphasis for speakers of languages such as English. It is also possible to observe use of the feet to perform the emphatic repetition of a beat, either in a furious stomp of the foot, or in a relaxed movement of the ankle while seated cross-legged.

Recurrent gestures

Recurrent gestures have meaning that relates to the pragmatic or discourse level of the interaction.

Some prototypical examples: a shrug with splayed upward hands for uncertainty, the sweeping of the hands away from the body while declaring you will *not* be cooking dinner, pinching the fingers together while emphasizing a detail that needs to be attended to.

Names for this category: pragmatic gestures (Kendon 2004: 285), recurrent gestures (Bressem and Müller 2014), interactive gestures (Bavelas et al. 1992).

Recurrent gestures have a form that occurs for speakers across a culture. These recurring forms relate to the structure of the interaction (the pragmatic level) rather than the meaning content (the semantic level). Because they have a pragmatic function rather than a semantic function, they are also known as pragmatic gestures. Laparle (2022) has created a typology of these gestures that operate at the discourse level. Key use of manual gestures include the introduction, organization, and removal of discourse topics within the interaction, and head gestures can be used to show that the speaker or listener is engaging or disengaging with the content of the discourse.

One example of a specific recurrent gesture is the pinching together the fingers, or using a handshape similar to the OK emblem gesture, suggesting a sense of precision or exactitude on behalf of the speaker (Kendon 2004: ch. 12; Neumann 2004; Lempert 2011). The precision is not necessarily in the speech content, but in the way the speaker is approaching it. Recurrent gestures often have overlap with the emblem repertoire of a cultural group, for example the OK emblem has an element of 'perfect' that is semantically linked to the concept of precision for the recurrent gesture, and has a similar form.

Recurrent gestures occur in particular linguistic or cultural areas, but because they also take their motivation from cognitive metaphors, we see similar recurrent gestures appear across different cultural groups. For example, we see that negation is indicated with some kind of trajectory away from the speaker in a wide range of cultures, including for Western languages such as German (Bressem and Müller 2014), French (Calbris 2011), Spanish (Teßendorf 2014), Italian (Kendon 2004), and English (Harrison 2010), but also in languages from other parts of the world including Savosavo (Papuan, Solomon Islands) (Bressem et al. 2017), Syuba (Tibeto-Burman, Nepal) (Gawne 2021), and Zulu, South Sotho, and Iscamtho (South Africa) (Brookes 2004).

Emblem gestures

Emblem gestures have a consistent form and meaning for a particular cultural group.

Some prototypical examples: thumbs up, peace sign/V for victory, nodding yes.

Names for this category: emblematic gestures (Efron 1941/1972), emblems (Ekman and Friesen 1969; McNeill 1992), symbolic gestures (Ricci Bitti 1992), autonomous gestures (Kendon 1983), quotable gestures (Kendon 2004).

The relationship between a stable form and a consistent meaning makes emblem gestures more word-like than many of the co-speech gestures discussed above. A 'thumbs up' is only a meaningful gesture for 'good' if the thumb is pointing upwards, if it points downwards you get 'bad', and it also has to be the thumb, rather than any other finger. Some examples of emblem gestures with widespread recognition include the thumbs up to mean 'good', the head nod to mean 'yes', and the shrug to mean 'I don't know'. Emblem gestures are often given names in areas where they are used. The word-like properties of emblem gestures make them more salient to people than more idiosyncratic co-speech gestures. While emblems are required to be well-formed, they do not have other features of language, for example they cannot combine readily into larger sentences. This is why emblems are more 'language-like' than the other categories of gesture discussed here. Gawne and Coooperrider (2024) provide a summary of existing documentation of emblem repertoires across cultures. This work is not evenly distributed across the world's cultures, but does highlight the rich diversity of emblem use.

The stable form–meaning relationship allows emblem gestures to be used independently of speech, which is why emblem gestures are treated as distinct from co-speech gestures in the gesture continuum introduced in Chapter 2. Although emblem gestures can have a consistent meaning even in the absence of speech, they are still frequently found in use with speech, and as such they are included in this chapter.

Emblem gestures only hold a specific meaning for a particular group of people. Emblem gestures can be meaningful for a small community, or for a larger cultural region. Common emblem gestures in Europe extend beyond specific linguistic regions, for example the 'good' meaning of the 'OK' gesture is found broadly across much of Europe, while it has a taboo meaning of 'orifice' in southern Italy and Greece, and the meaning 'zero' in Belgium, France, and northern Spain (Morris et al. 1979: 114). Emblem gestures can be very durable in their use, in some cases remaining stable as the languages around them change and evolve. The head toss found in southern Italy is thought to be a cultural import from Greece in the third century BCE (Kendon 2004: 338–9). At the other end of the size scale, small communities can also have rich inventories of emblem gestures; Brookes (2004) provides rich and robust documentation of over 100 gestures used in a multilingual township in South Africa.

While there are many emblem gestures that have existed for so long that their origins are obscured for us, there are some semiotic pathways to their creation that we can observe. The first is that they can have an iconic origin; the 'finger heart' made by crossing your thumb and index finger popularized by Korean pop musicians in the mid 2010s is an iconic representation of a heart shape. The second pathway is metaphoric; the 'thumbs up' to mean 'good' is part of a larger cultural metaphor of 'up is good'. The third resource for emblem gestures is emergent bodily action; the proposed motivation for the head shake to mean 'no' is the sideways movement of the head as a child to refuse food (Darwin 1872, although see Kettner and Carpendale 2013 for a refutation of this theory).

Applying categories

Above, we have looked at some of the major categories found in the Gesture Studies literature with clear, prototypical examples. These are summarised in Table 2. Although McNeill's gesture categories are often cited and highly influential, not every category McNeill proposed has achieved particular longevity. The category of cohesives (McNeill 1992: 16–18) was proposed to account for the way gesture can be used to bring cohesion to temporally distant parts of the narrative through use of the same gesture. McNeill acknowledged a cohesive could be any of the existing categories of gesture, and that this was an additional discourse

Table 2 Summary of gesture categories

	Definition	Examples
Iconic	Depict the physical properties of things in the world	Indicating the size of a fish, depicting how quickly a plane flew by, demonstrating how fluffy a cat is
Metaphoric	Depict abstract concepts as having physical properties	Moving hand upward to show improvement, indicating ahead to refer to tomorrow, placing two arguments on the left and right of your gesture space
Deictic	Indicate a place or object	Pointing at a door in the room, pointing towards the direction of the city, indicating with your head where someone was sitting at their desk yesterday
Beat	A repetitive action used for emphasis	The 'don't you do that!' scold with the extended wagging index finger, the gestures used by politicians to emphasize a point
Recurrent	Relate to the pragmatic or discourse level of the interaction	A shrug with splayed upward hands for uncertainty
Emblem	Stable form and meaning for a specific group	Thumbs up, peace sign/V for victory, nodding yes

function. For this reason, cohesion has remained something that is a general function of gesture, but not something discussed as a distinct gestural category. A second category that has not found its way into the general research literature on gesture is that of 'butterworths', those gestures that are used during a speech failure, such as searching for a word. McNeill named these after Brian Butterworth, a British neuropsychologist who had studied these kinds of gestures (Butterworth and Beattie 1978). While the use of gesture with pauses and hesitations continues to be studied (e.g. Kısa 2022), this term has not lasted.

In spontaneous use, gestures can demonstrate a complex blending of categories. In fact, gestures are rarely just one category, and instead show a complex blend of functions that are grounded in the specific context. For example, a pointing handshape might be used to indicate the direction and also the iconic properties of a bumpy trajectory of an airplane lifting off in bad weather, or someone might use a precision grip with a biphasic beat structure to really emphasize the meticulous nature of their plans.

There are some particularly common blends of categories that you might encounter. The first is that of beat gestures with other categories. One of the key features of beat gestures is their biphasic repetitive stroke. This means that they can blend easily with any other category to add emphasis to the message; to really emphasize the direction you are pointing, the affirmation of a thumbs up, or the excellent size of a wheel of cheese you just purchased. As Kendon (2004: 103) notes, beat gestures turn up in blends with other categories with some ubiquity. Another common combination is that of a deictic gesture with some kind of iconic information, perhaps an indication of the manner of motion as well as the direction. These categories are not mutually exclusive in their performance, instead they are a helpful tool in analysing the range of functional contributions gestures make in communication.

Conclusion

Categories of gesture draw on both the function and the form of a gesture in its context of use. There are some categories of gesture that are commonly used by gesture researchers. Iconic gestures depict the physical properties of things in the world. This can be done through modelling, depicting, or enacting, and can involve either an observer or character viewpoint. Metaphoric gestures depict abstract concepts as having physical properties. They use the same imagistic resources as iconic gestures, but for the concrete representation of abstract concepts rather than physical entities. These metaphors are often culturally-pervasive cognitive metaphors that show up across both speech and gesture. Deictic gestures indicate a place or object. These can be real or imaginary, present or absent. Beat gestures are a repetitive action used for emphasis. A beat aligns with the phonological rhythms of speech, and has a complex biphasic stroke. Recurrent gestures relate to the pragmatic or discourse level of the interaction. These often draw on cognitive metaphors and are culturally pervasive. Emblems are gestures with a stable form and meaning for a specific group. This makes them more 'word like' and able to be used without speech than the other categories of gesture discussed here. Gestures can often exhibit dimensions of multiple categories.

Further reading and resources

The first section of the *Cambridge Handbook of Gesture Studies* contains chapters on different gestural types, which includes all of the categories discussed here, including subcategories and variations in approach to gesture categorization.

The Tom Scott video *Why Do We Move Our Hands When We Talk?*[1] provides a lightning three-minute introduction to the topic of gesture, including the major categories discussed here. For a longer informal introduction to gesture categories, Gretchen McCulloch's Because Internet (2019) uses them as a tool for exploring the different uses of emojis alongside text in online communication.

---

[1] https://youtu.be/gGMkHzWXjI8

4

Gesture across cultures and languages

Where there is language, there is gesture. People across all languages and cultures gesture, and this ubiquity results in some common features of gesture that we have looked at in the previous two chapters. Alongside these commonalities, we can also see distinct use of gesture in different populations. In this chapter we explore some of the factors that lead to variation in gesture across different groups of people.

These influences are grouped under three major topics, the first is cultural influence. This includes examination of how people use the gestural space available to them, how gesture use is influenced by a culture-specific understanding of politeness, and the spread of culture-specific emblem gestures. The second is cognitive influence on gestures. In this section we look at the literature on the way different groups conceptualize spatial relationships, and how this affects gesture use. We look at how spatial metaphors for time influence gesture use. The third and final topic is the influence of language structure on gestural production. In this section we will look at the way the semantics and syntax of verbs in different languages influence the shape of iconic gestures.

I have selected this order for the discussion of variation because of the different time scales of influence and affect involved. Cultural influences shape gestural preferences from the moment of acquisition onwards. It is possible to shift between conventions if you move between cultural groups. At the other end of the scale, the languages you speak appear to influence gesture production much more at the point of conceptualization of thought for speaking.

Gesture. Lauren Gawne, Oxford University Press. © Lauren Gawne (2025).
DOI: 10.1093/9780198951377.003.0004

Culture influencing gesture

Human language, including gesture, is influenced by the cultural context in which people use it. Cultural regions can overlap with linguistic boundaries, but this is not necessarily the case. A particular cultural space may spread across many languages, or may comprise a subset of speakers of a language. In this section we look at examples of both possibilities.

We explore three different types of cultural influence. The first is differences in the way the gesture space is used in different cultures. The second is the influence of cross-cultural variation in politeness on the use of gesture. For the third we look at variation in culturally-transmitted gestures.

Cultural convention and the gesture space

In Chapter 2 we explored the concept of the gesture space, the area around the body people use to gesture. The extent to which the gesture space is used in communication appears to be culturally motivated. This was described by Efron (1941/1972), who observed differences in the use of the gesture space between Southern Italian and Eastern European Jewish immigrants in New York City. Efron used film recordings to generate his findings, a highly novel method at the time. He noted that first generation Italian American men tended to gesture in the periphery of the gesture space, moving the entire arm from the shoulder, and made use of the lateral plane out to their sides. In contrast, Jewish men more often gestured in the central gesture space, moving only from the elbow and wrist joints, and tended to make more use of the vertical and sagittal planes. Articulation from the shoulder meant the Italian participants made larger gestures that used more of the gesture space. The children and grandchildren of both groups of migrants, who were raised speaking American English alongside any heritage languages, did not show the same use of the gesture space, and gestured more like each other than either group of their immigrant forebears, converging into the space between the more restricted Eastern European gesturers and the expansive space used by the Italians. Informally, Efron noted that those with stronger connection to their ethnic background still gestured more in line with the original immigrant cohort (1941/1972: 154), suggesting that the process of changing gestural practice across generations is complex, contextual, and individual.

Politeness and gesture

In the previous section, we explored how general cultural conventions influence gestural frequency, gesture size, and use of the gesture space. But we also know that use of the gesture space can be influenced by specific cultural motivations. One of these motivations is politeness. Cultural variation in what people consider to be polite can affect people's choices in interaction (Brown and Levinson 1987). Researchers looking at gesture use across cultures have used the framework of politeness theory to understand some of the variation in gesture repertoires between cultures. We will focus on research exploring nodding, pointing, and taboo emblems.

The use of head nodding during conversation is mediated by cultural expectations of what makes a polite interlocutor. English and Japanese speakers both use vertical affirmative nodding when they are the addressee in a conversation. This is a back-channelling function to indicate attention to the speaker and intent to continue listening. While English speakers nod almost exclusively during an identifiable pause at the end of a clause, Japanese speakers nod in far more contexts, including in response to sentence-final particles, pauses at any point in the utterance, and speaker head movements (Maynard 1986). It is perhaps unsurprising given the wider variety of contexts of use, but nodding is far more frequent in the Japanese data than the American English speaker data of Maynard's study.

Both speaker and addressee in Japanese interactions use nodding as a way to manage whose turn it is to speak (Maynard 1987). Kita and Ide (2007) noted a similar difference in nodding distribution for Japanese and English speakers and suggested that the proposition-internal nods in particular provide a flexible way for Japanese speakers to establish and maintain a social bond. It is not that English speakers do not manage turn taking and relationships, but that they do not place the same emphasis on using nodding as a strategy.

When it comes to pointing, issues of politeness tend to focus on actions that are prohibited. There are, broadly, two types of prohibition on pointing; a prohibition on what can be pointed at, and a prohibition on how pointing can be performed. Both of these types of prohibition stem from the fact that pointing is seen as threatening. Documented prohibitions on pointing come from a range of cultures, and vary in terms of the target of the taboo. In Zulu communities, there are prohibitions on pointing at objects associated with the ancestors, and pointing to crops, which will make them die and may cause your arm to become diseased (Raum 1973: 437). The Kédang of Indonesia have a prohibition on pointing at Ursa Major, or small young pumpkins (Barnes 1973: 612). The Vezo of Madagascar have a prohibition on pointing at large sea creatures (whales, sharks, and giant octopuses) with an extended index finger (Astuti 1995: 49). A taboo that occurs across a wide range of cultures is a prohibition on pointing at rainbows. Blust (2021) documents examples of this prohibition from 124 cultural groups (including Kédang speakers, who include this taboo alongside the constellation and pumpkins). Another commonly cited pointing taboo is a prohibition on pointing at other people. Interactional data from Western contexts notes that even with this considered a taboo, there is not actually a particular scarcity of pointing at people (Healy 2012; Fenlon et al. 2019). What does appear to change when it comes to pointing at people is the way that the pointing occurs. Which brings us to the other type of pointing prohibition; modification of the way pointing is done.

The taboo on pointing at people appears to manifest as modified forms of pointing. In one study with Polish speakers, this included far fewer index finger points, and more pointing done with an open palm or eye gaze (Jarmołowicz-Nowikow 2015: 90). In one set of English-speaking interview data, participants were more likely to use an open palm point for their addressee than other entities (Fenlon et al. 2019: 12). The BSL data from the same study does not show the same preference for this open palm, instead the index finger was strongly preferred, which is the grammatical form of pronominal reference for a single addressee in the language. In some Australian Aboriginal groups, the prohibition on pointing at people is active when showing circumspection about particular kin relations. The prohibition can be worked around using the fist, or by pointing with the knee or elbow.

Pointing form taboos extend beyond pointing at people. A study on Malaysian direction-giving noted the use of pointing with the thumb as a common strategy, where the thumb is held forwards above a clenched fist (Mechraoui and Noor 2017: 90). In another direction-giving study in Ghana, Kita and Essegbey (2001) looked at politeness constraints on the use of the left hand. In Ghana, and other West African countries, there is a taboo on the use of the left hand for a range of interactional actions, including giving and receiving, as well as for actions like eating and drinking. This also includs a preference for using the left hand to point; 60 per cent of Ghanaians interviewed in Kita and Essegbey's (2001) paper thought that left-hand pointing was impolite. In their documentation of public use of pointing to give directions, Kita and Essegbey noted that fewer left-hand gestures were used compared to similar data collected in other countries, with a preference for right-hand use even in contexts where the right arm had to cross over the body and it would have been less gestural effort to use the left hand. The left hand was usually held low, out of sight, or alternatively, the left hand could be used if the left and right hand were held together in a two-handed point, which was commonly observed. When the left hand was used, these gestures were notably different to left-hand points, usually held low in the gesture space and consisting of little more than a flick of the wrist. All of these variations on the form of pointing in particular cultural contexts share what Cooperrider (2020: 22) calls an apparent attempt to 'defang finger pointing'.

One final area of politeness and gesture relates to those gestures which are considered, because of their culture-specific meaning, to be taboo to perform. Some gestures are rude in particular cultures regardless of who performs them. The raised middle finger is rude across large areas of Western Europe, so much so that many people in this cultural area often avoid using the middle finger to point with. The gesture commonly known as the OK gesture in the same area of Western Europe (thumb and index in a ring with the other fingers splayed) is performed as an orifice-related taboo in southern Italy and Greece (Morris et al. 1979), as well as parts of the Middle East and South America (Morris 1994), and is considered offensive when performed in these cultural areas.

Culturally-transmitted gestures

Emblems have a stable relationship between form and meaning and can be used communicatively without speech, and are transmitted culturally. We saw above how the OK gesture is fine in Western Europe, but taboo in Greece and parts of Italy. There are also some other gestural forms that are also deeply linked to culture. In this section, we will look briefly at the cultural transmission of emblems, and also explore cultural variation in the shape of deictic gestures, and the use of culturally-transmitted gestures in art.

The distribution of emblem gestures does not follow linguistic boundaries. In Morris et al.'s (1979) survey of emblem gestures across Europe we can see there are three broad cultural zones, south west Europe (Italy and Spain), south east Europe (Greece and Turkey), and northern Europe (Britain and Scandinavia) (Kendon 1981: 146). These gesture ecologies are areas of long, sustained linguistic and cultural contact. Emblem gestures can continue to be transmitted and maintain their form and meaning even as languages change around them.

Emblems are not the only gestures where cultural transmission influences the performance of a gesture. Deictic gestures across human cultures share a general form through extension of one part of the body towards the referent location. We saw above that finger pointing is often subject to cultural prohibitions, but even when it is not, culture influences the form of pointing used (Figure 7). In a survey of six languages, Wilkins (2003) noted that while index finger pointing is ubiquitous in English, it is not the preferred form of pointing for the Barai (Papua New Guinea) community, and only infrequently used in Awtuw (Papua New Guinea) and Kuna (Panama) communities. In these three communities, lip pointing was the ubiquitous form of deictic gesture used, which is not part of the typical deictic repertoire for Western speakers of English. For speakers of Arrernte (Australia), index finger and lip

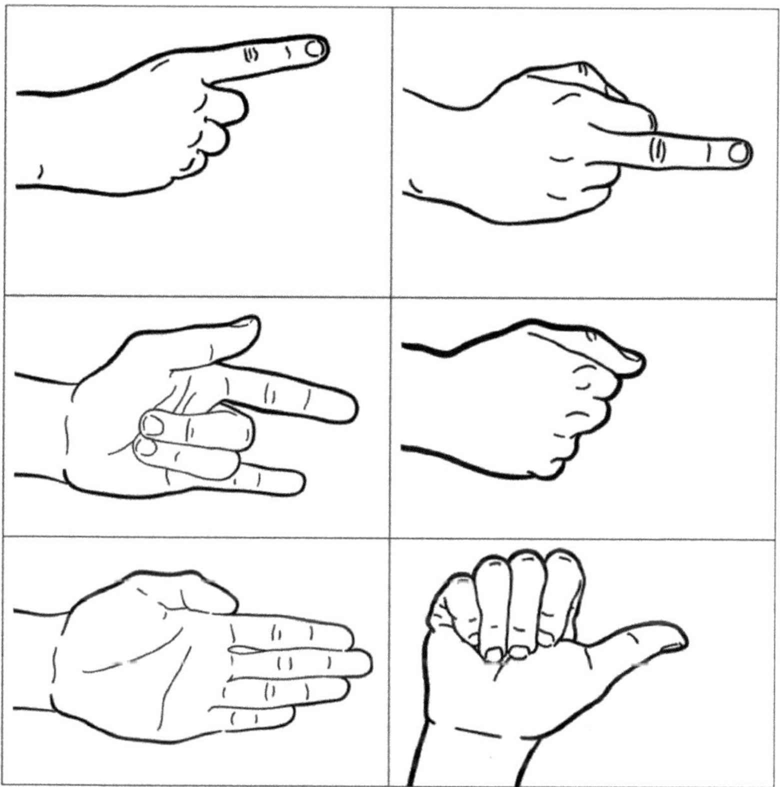

Figure 7 Some of the handshape variation in pointing
Based on artwork by Lucy Maddox

pointing are both common, but have different functions; lip pointing has more informal use and can be used for more secretive reference to a location. Cooperrider et al. (2018b) also noted variation between American English speakers, who overwhelmingly preferred hand pointing, and Yupno (Papua New Guinea) speakers who used a mix of gestures performed with the head and the hands. A Western preference for hand gestures has until recent decades perpetuated a focus on manual gestures as the prototypical form of deixis, while in reality there are different preferences in different cultures. Even in cultures where index pointing might be the default, there is still a lot of variation; in an exploration of pointing in Naples, Kendon and Versante (2003) noted that speakers will use thumb pointing for ease of indicating a location behind the speaker, an open palm prone for a form of pointing and display, and an open palm vertical when the referent is being ascribed some attribute.

Cultural transmission of gesture can also require gestural literacy for participation in a range of art forms across cultures. *Mudras* are the handshapes used in Hindu and Buddhist prayer, sculpture and painting, communicating rich theological meaning to those literate in the traditions. For example, the *Abhayamudrā* is the right hand held with palm facing outwards and all fingers extended upwards and held together. It is used as a mudra of teaching, granting the absence of fear (Saunders 1985: 55). Gestural literacy is also important in the Western art tradition, which makes use of ritual handshapes and postures, which are explicitly learnt and deployed across different art forms (Morris 2019). For example, the gesture of benediction with the index and middle fingers raised, has a long history in Western Christian traditions, and is often used in representations of Jesus Christ or the saints. In the Eastern Orthodox tradition the gesture tends to have the ring finger and thumb in a circle, and the pinky extended, giving the gesture a different shape. In non-religious iconography, the eighteenth-century fad of portraits of men posed with a hand tucked into their jacket is influenced by Classical sculpture. In the earlier period it was a way to show that you were a dignified orator who used arguments instead of flashy performance to win people over, which appealed to Napoleon and people of his era who wanted to signal they were genteel and restrained.

Beyond religion, all art that involves the human body requires a culturally-specific understanding of the role of gesture. This is as true for the highly stylized performance of Kabuki theatre in Japan, where the use of masks places even more communicative responsibility on the gestures, as it is for the move towards naturalism in twentieth-century Western cinema. Dances from different regions of India draw on *mudras*, that share a name with, but are distinct from the religions forms. These handshapes can be used to act out social interactions in the dance, such as asking questions, scolding, or listening, or to perform actions, such as braiding hair or to represent objects such as the moon or clouds. The gendered nature of the use of some mudras allow for role-play across genders in a number of dance traditions (Bagchi 2010).

Cognition influencing gesture

Some elements of the culture in which we are raised are so influential that they appear to affect the way we conceptualize the world. We have seen above how culture can influence the form of gestures, but in this section we will explore how culture and language influences cognition, which then has a subsequent effect on the way people gesture. We will examine the literature in three related areas. The first is the influence of spatial cognition on gesture, and then how that spatial cognition can extend into the metaphoric domain, particularly in relation to metaphors for time. Finally we will look at other ways cultural metaphors affect cognition, which results in variation in gesture use.

Spatial cognition and gesture

Different languages use different ways of talking about direction and location in space, which have flow-on effects for communication, including gesture. We can divide these approaches into two broad categories. The first uses relative frames of reference. This is seen in the English terms 'left' and 'right'. If an apple is to the right of a cup of coffee, then from someone else's perspective it might be more correct to say it is on the left. The reference is relative to the speaker and other features of the context, which is why I might check to clarify if it is my right or your right. The other way spatial reference can be done is through absolute frames of reference. These frames of reference do not change for any of the people in the conversation. Referring to our apple again, using absolute referents we might say the apple is north of the cup. As well as cardinal directions (which are oriented in relation to the path of the sun rather than magnetic poles), absolute systems can use key geographic features, such as seaward and landward or up/down a mountain. Of course, these absolute systems are not infinitely absolute, and only extend as far as the relevant geographic features, but they are absolute in contrast to relative systems and sufficient for the communities that use them.

As is evident from the two examples above, English has words for both relative (left/right) and absolute (north/south/etc.) spatial orientation.

Although we have the terminology to talk in absolute terms, when it comes to discussing the relationship of anything other than major geographical features, such as our apple and coffee, we use and think in terms of relative orientation. This is not the case for all languages. For example speakers of Guugu Yimithirr in Queensland, Australia and Tzeltal speakers in Tenejapa, Mexico use an absolute reference system even for the small-scale relation between two objects (Levinson and Wilkins 2006). Guugu Yimithirr speakers use a quadrant system broadly analogous to cardinal directions, while Tzeltal speakers use an up/downhill system. Although these systems show up in the word choices people make, they are actually much more pervasive and embedded in the way people think about spatial relationships. It is for this reason that we talk about the cognitive influence on gesture rather than linguistic influence on gesture.

Having to refer to the relationship between objects or places in absolute space means that speakers of these languages pay much more attention to this property of their world. Levinson and Wilkins's (2006) work demonstrates the cognitive effect of this on a pattern matching task, but we also see gestural evidence for the way this form of spatial thinking influences people's gestures. Haviland (2000) examines two recordings of a story about a capsized boat, told by a Guugu Yimithirr speaker who uses an absolute spatial reference system. In one recording the speaker is facing west, and in another he is facing north. In the two different tellings, the speaker changes the orientation of the gesture depicting the boat rolling in the ocean so that the gesture is consistently performed along the same absolute orientation as the original event, even in tellings several years apart. In this example, and many others, gesture provides evidence for spatial thinking that is independent of the linguistic content of the narrative, giving 'insight into another level of mental life' (Levinson 2003: 216).

Spatial metaphor, time, and gesture

The category of metaphoric gestures was introduced in Chapter 3. As well as more spontaneous metaphors that might arise in a particular interaction, there are many metaphors that are so deeply entrenched and culturally-transmitted that they have profound influences on how we talk and think about the world (Lakoff and Johnson 1980). Researchers have observed how these metaphors influence the way people gesture, even when there is no overt use of the metaphor in the accompanying speech. This means that sometimes gesture provides us with evidence that the metaphor is still being used in the process of thinking, even without evidence from the accompanying linguistic content.

If you made a video about October and were gesturing ahead of your-self, and mentioned something about August and indicated that August was somewhere behind you, I would guess without any other detail that the recording took place in September. That is because English speakers, and speakers of many European languages, have a sense of time where the future is in front of the body and the past is behind, on a sagittal timeline (Figure 8). This spatial orientation of time is also evident in our speech, where we talk about 'putting the past behind us' and 'looking for-ward to next summer'. Sometimes, in this spatiotemporal metaphor, we are actively moving along a timeline, and sometimes we are stationary while time moves around us.

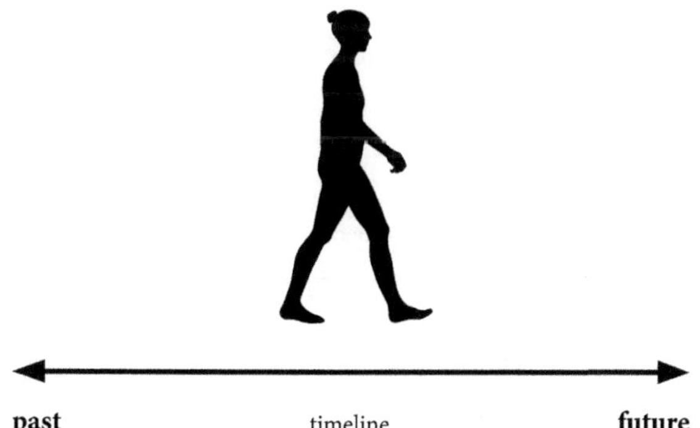

Figure 8 A representation of the future in front metaphor
Image by Lucy Maddox

Gesture provides us with evidence that these lexical constructions have cognitive spatial reality, and allows us to track active cogni-tion that uses these metaphors even when there is no accompanying lexical evidence. Time (famously) does not have a physical dimension, and in order to make it approachable, we have mapped this abstract domain into a physical one. This is not just true for specific temporal events, but more broadly too; Cienki (2008) examined the genre of soviet statues of Lenin, with his arm outstretched in front of him, pointing with an index finger, or palm open and fingers extended, metaphorically gesturing towards the bright future of communism. Even though the monument-building days of twentieth-century communism are well in our past, we still clearly read the metaphor of the gesture.

This is not the only mapping of time in many Western cultures; we also have a sense of time on a line in front of us, with events moving horizontally from the left to the right. This metaphor is not motivated by our bodies, but our writing system, which starts on the left and moves across the page (and therefore across time) to the right (Figure 9). Again, thanks to the ubiquity of literacy, this metaphoric approach to time as linear and spatial feels unremarkable to a reader of this book, even though we do not have this as a pervasive lexical metaphor ('putting the past to the left of us'). English speakers use both future-forward and future-right conceptualizations of time when gesturing (Casasanto and Jasmin 2012), but tend to use the horizontal space more when talking about the sequence of events. The fact that there is a shared preference for this mental

Figure 9 A representation of the future to the right metaphor
Image by Lucy Maddox

representation of time in space that does not show up in the lexicon is one of the reasons this is a cognitive influence rather than a linguistic one.

Other cultures have other ways of conceptualizing time in space. Speakers of Aymara (an Indigenous language of the Andean highlands) conceptualize time with the future behind them and the past in front (Figure 10), a reversal of the spatial orientation common in Western temporal metaphors. This metaphor certainly has some merit— we cannot see what is in the future, but we bear witness to what has already gone before. In an analysis of a series of informal conversational narrative video recordings from Aymara speakers, Núñez and Sweetser (2006) use a range of examples to demonstrate how the speaker's gestures map to this metaphor. For example, one bilingual speaker referred to '*el tiempo antes*' (the before times) with his right hand raised and pointing forward with his index finger as high as his face, in what Núñez and Sweetser call an 'emphatic' gesture (2006: 428). While these metaphors are robust for speakers, they are also fragile in their transmission. In their work with Aymara communities Núñez and Sweetser recorded Aymara speakers, who tended to be older, as well as younger Aymara people who were more likely to be Spanish speakers or bilinguals. Only the Aymara speakers and bilinguals used

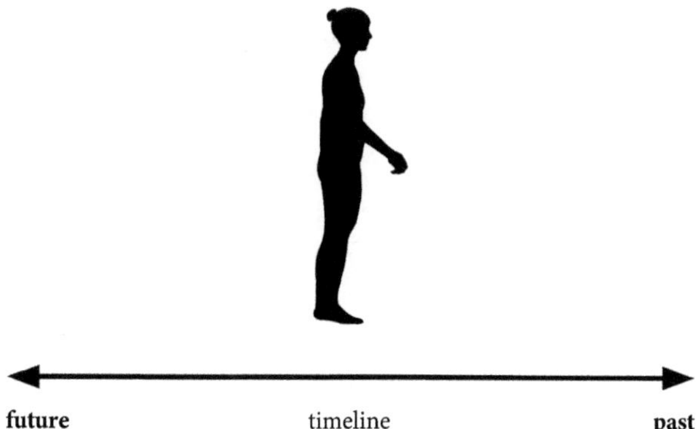

Figure 10 A representation of the future behind metaphor
Image by Lucy Maddox

this metaphor in their gesture or speech, with younger Aymara now speaking Spanish and using a future-in-front model in both speech and gesture. Aymara is not the only language that is reported to have a past-in-front model. de la Fuente et al. (2014) discussed a tendency to gesture with the past in front for Arabic speakers in Morocco. Unlike in Aymara, Arabic has a preference for speaking using the opposite metaphor, with the future in front of the speaker (a finding replicated by Gu 2018).

Chinese speakers, like English speakers, have been demonstrated to have multiple spatial metaphors when talking about time. There is a vertical metaphor where earlier events are higher up and later events are lower. This metaphor is lexically encoded in terms like 上周/*shàng zhōu* 'last week' (lit. 'above week') and 下周/*xià zhōu* 'next week' (lit. 'below week') (from Gu 2018: 29). Not all temporal gestures produced by Chinese speakers are vertical; Chui (2011) analysed examples that showed horizontal spatial metaphors for time were also used in Chinese conversation. In a series of experiments, Gu (2018) unpacks the complexity of these multiple metaphors and paints a picture of the complexity of cognitive spatiotemporal models. Chinese speakers are statistically more likely to use vertial time gestures while speaking Chinese and more likely to use words with the vertical sense, but they will still use vertical gestures with spatially neutral lexical items in Chinese (2018: 37). When studying gesture use by Chinese speakers of English as a second language, participants were more likely to gesture vertically if the lexical item was vertical in Chinese even if it was neutral in English, but did still also use vertical gestures across a range of English words (2018: 39), showing cross-linguistic transfer of the cognitive metaphor. In a perception task, Chinese speakers also preferred vertical gestures more than English speakers did (2018: 47). Gu (2018), in replicating de la Fuente et al.'s (2014) work, found that Chinese speakers in their perception of horizontal gestures had a preference for past in front. This preference was not as strong as for Moroccan Arabic speakers, but stronger than for Spanish speakers. The preference could also be manipulated by the metaphor conditions used to prime the Chinese participants, those primed with a 'future in front' metaphor condition were more likely to orient towards that, as did those in the 'past in front' metaphor condition, with the use of neutral words and conditions somewhere between the two (Gu 2018: 76). Gu's work shows us that the way people access and use spatiotemporal metaphors in both words and gestures is complex and nuanced. Rather than ascribing speakers of languages like Chinese to single systems and making claims about cognition, we still need to do a lot of work to understand the nuance of these metaphoric gestures and their role in cognition (Chen and O'Seaghdha 2013).

Cultural preference for absolute spatial reference can also show up in metaphors for time. Speakers of Kuuk Tyayorre have an absolute spatial reference system based on the orientation of the sun, and have been observed pointing to the east (sunrise) to refer to the past (Gaby 2012). Yupno speakers in Papua New Guinea have an absolute spatial system that uses an environment-based topography of the local mountains. In discussing temporal events, Yupno speakers use a metaphor where the past is downhill and the future is uphill from the speaker in both speech and gesture (Núñez et al. 2012).

There are also a small number of reported cases where a particular cultural group does not appear to use metaphorical gestures. In a study on Yucatec Maya, Le Guen and Balam (2012) found only a broad opposition between 'current time' located near the body, and 'remote time' mapped further out into the gesture space, with no contrast of past and future and no metaphorical timeline of events. The speakers do not make use of the local geocentric absolute spatial system in their gestures, instead Le Guen and Balam (2012) argue that the gestures are more in keeping with the Yucatec Mayan understanding of time as cyclical. Yélî Dnye (PNG) speakers do not appear to have a shared cultural representation of time on spatial dimensions, either in casual speech or experimental conditions, and by extension do not have a gestural representation of time that is spatially meaningful (Levinson and Majid 2013).

It is one thing to observe variation in the way communities gesture about time, and the spatial metaphors that they draw on, it is another thing to ascribe reason to their different metaphors. de la Fuente et al. (2014) suggest it is a cultural attitude towards time that might motivate the past in front orientation, with Moroccan Arabic speakers having a strong orientation to the past. Gu (2018), in replicating the work of de la Fuente et al., documented cultural orientation towards past or future for Moroccan Arabic, Mandarin, and Spanish speakers, and found a positive correlation between past-orientation and use of past-in-front temporal gestures. Whether there is a cultural relationship, or something more practical like the influence of the directionality of the writing system, the motivation for this cultural variation is not always clear.

Cognitive metaphor and gesture

Spatiotemporal metaphors are not the only cognitive metaphors for which we have gestural evidence. We see a convergence on cognitive metaphors across independent cultural groups, because the cognition of all humans is constrained by the physical experience of moving through the world in corporeal form. For example, similarity has been noted across cultures in the presentation of the palm upwards, often with some lateral movement, that indicates 'absence of knowledge' (Cooperrider et al. 2018a). This is most readily accessible to English speakers and other Western cultures in the use of the hands in a 'shrug' emblem, but similar actions with similar meanings have been found in African and Asian cultural contexts as well as being used as a grammatical resource in signed languages from these areas. Cooperrider et al. (2018a: 12) put forward the possibility that the open hands are showing the person does not possess knowledge on the topic. This potential metaphoric motivation could help explain why this gesture is found across such a wide range of languages and cultures.

The cultural context of an individual does not just have to be at the level of the language spoken; there has been work looking at the use of metaphor in particular subcultures and professional domains as well. Calbris (2008) demonstrated how former French Prime Minister Lionel Jospin would use his left hand and left gesture space to represent colleagues and concepts from the political Left, extending the spatial metaphor into the gestural domain even when the context was not overtly about their place in the political chamber. There are also examples of how mathematicians use metaphorical concepts of movement in their discussion of abstract mathematics (Núñez 2008), and linguists represent abstract entities such as verbs and sentences as having physical properties while teaching linguistics (Mittelberg 2008).

Idiosyncratic metaphoric gestures can also emerge from the particular conversational context, and hold over extended periods of discourse. Müller (2008) illustrates this through analysis of a conversation between two young adults, Lea and Gregor, who have just finished tertiary education and are considering their first jobs, and whether this sets their life on a particular course. Together they settle on a metaphor of a railway track, with Lea arguing that your first job does not confine you to a single track, and Gregor disagreeing. This is a 'local establishment' (Müller 2008: 232) of a metaphor that is carried through Georg's argument, across multiple lines of conversation and eight different gesture phrases. In fact, he finishes his argument not with words, but by gesturing with his right hand straight ahead while the forearm is held with his left hand, illustrating his argument that the job has set a single track that affords no switching.

Language influencing gesture

Above we have seen how culture and cognition can influence language. This could theoretically come about regardless of the actual language spoken by members of a cultural group (we will look specifically at the issue of gesture transfer into a second language in Chapter 5). In this section, the focus is specifically on those elements of the structure of the language that influence the structure of gestures.

Verb structure

One of the best studied examples of the influence of language on gesture is the cross-linguistic representation of motion events. Before we get to the gestures, let's briefly examine the different ways that languages can structure motion events grammatically. Languages vary with regard to whether verbs focus on the manner in which an action takes place, or the path that the action takes (Talmy 1985). A language such as English has lots of verbs like 'roll', 'crawl', and 'swing', which emphasize the way something happened (the manner) and uses additional linguistic elements to describe the trajectory (path) of something rolling 'down', or 'away'. Another language with a focus on manner is Estonian (Finno-Ugric), with verbs such as *lonkima* 'stroll', *jooksma* 'run', and *kihutama* 'race'. In contrast, Spanish has verbs that tend to focus on path: *entrar* ('enter'), *salir* ('go out'), subir ('go up'), with the manner included as additional information. English 'she ran in' translates as *ella entró corriendo*, which is more literally 'she entered running'. We can think of languages like English and Estonian as 'manner-verb' languages, and language like Spanish, and others including Turkish and Japanese, as 'path-verb' languages.

Kita and Özyürek (2003) examined motion event gestures for speakers of English, a manner-verb language and Turkish and Japanese, which are path-verb languages. Speakers of English were far more likely to include both path and manner information in their gestures, while speakers of the path-focused languages were just as likely to only indicate path, or show path and manner in two distinct gestural actions, one after the other. English speakers are not obliged to always merge manner and path into a single iconic gesture. In a follow-on study, English speakers were asked to describe short videos where some of the actions encouraged speakers to describe the manner and path in two separate clauses (Kita et al. 2007). When this happened, it also changed how they package the gestures to look more like gestures used by the Turkish and Japanese speakers in the earlier study, with fewer gestures that combined path and manner. Özyürek et al. (2005) used the same stimuli set and found that Turkish and English speakers are more likely to have similar gestures that do not combine path and manner when the stimuli represents distinct phases for these two elements. These additional studies shows that the difference between languages is not due to cognitive differences between speakers of these languages, but has to do with how each of these languages package these events, and the way gestures are packaged up with speech in the cognitive process.

We also know that the difference in gesture performance is most likely an influence of the grammatical structure of the language, rather than a learned behaviour, because blind Turkish and English speakers demonstrate the same gestural patterns (Özçalışkan et al. 2016). Turkish, Japanese, and English speaking three- and four-year-olds showed similar tendencies as adult speakers of these languages (Allen et al. 2007), although these preferences may not be robust until much later; with Özyürek et al. (2008) finding that adult-like usage stabilizes around nine years of age for English and Turkish speaking children. All of this work makes the iconic representation of motion one of the most robustly studied elements of how the structure of different languages shapes the performance of gestures during speech.

Semantics influencing gesture

In addition to the structure of language influencing our gestures, the semantics of the language we speak also affect our gestural production. Continuing the discussion of motion evens, in their work on path and manner verbs, Kita and Özyürek (2003) examined the cross-linguistic differences with regard to the action of swinging, which occurred in the video stimulus they used when one of the characters used a rope to swing from one building across to the other. English has the verb 'swing', which conveys the arcing manner of the action. There is no verb with the same semantics in Turkish or Japanese. All the English speaking participants in the study used the word 'swing' for the action, and the accompanying gesture mostly included the arcing trajectory. The Japanese and Turkish speaking participants used more generic verbs that would translate into English words such as 'jump' or 'go', and were also more likely to use a straight line gesture. The lexical resources in each language influenced the performance of gesture when describing the event.

Conclusion

Gestures show variation in use across groups. This variation can be motivated by influences from culture, cognition, or language. With regard to culture, gestures may vary depending on cultural convention around how the gesture space is used. Politeness and taboo can also affect which gestures are performed, and there are culturally transmitted gestures, particularly emblems. There are also cognitive influences on gesture. The spatial reference system used by a cultural group can affect iconic representation of events in gestural form. Metaphors for time using spatial features affects how we gesture about events, and there are also other metaphors, both persistent and idiosyncratic, that provide a cognitive frame that affects our gestures. Finally, the structure of the language we speak can have an effect on the way gestures are produced. This has been extensively studied for the structure of motion verbs, and we also see an influence of semantics on gesture forms.

Further reading and resources

A comprehensive summary of the work conducted on the cross-cultural variation in gesture is provided in Kita (2009). As you may have noticed across this chapter, Kita has been involved in key research across a number of these topics, including the influence of cultural pragmatics and linguistic structures on gesture production.

In a shortform essay for *Aeon*, Kensy Cooperrider teases out the tension between the cultural variation in gesture use, and its iconic properties: From pointing to nodding: Is gesture a universal language?[1] Cooperrider has written a range of essays, linked on his website,[2] on topics related to the cultural diversity of gesture, including forms of pointing, pointing taboos, and different spatial and temporal reference systems.

[1] https://aeon.co/essays/from-pointing-to-nodding-is-gesture-a-universal-language
[2] http://kensycooperrider.com/writing

5

Gesture acquisition and use

Who are gestures for? Are they something that we use to convey our intention to our audience, or are they something we use to help ourselves construct our thoughts and speech? In this chapter we will look at evidence for both functions of gesture, which helps us build a more complex picture of the role of gesture in communication. Some gestures may play an intentional communicative role for the audience, while others might serve a cognitive role for the speaker as they put their thoughts together into language; a distinction Cooperrider (2017) refers to as 'foreground gestures' (deliberate, for the audience) and 'background gestures' (not necessarily for the audience, possibly helpful for speaker processing). It is worth stating very clearly that we will not be coming to a one-or-the-other conclusion here—these are not mutually-exclusive possibilities. Rather than thinking of gestures as either just for speakers or just for audience, they have a multi-faceted role in interaction. We will also look at the use of gesture in language learning across the lifespan; we will start with the earliest stages of language development with first language acquisition, before looking at the way gesture changes as we learn languages later in life.

So far we have looked at commonalities of gesture performance and categorization, as well as variation that arises between groups of people. When we look at the use of gestures, for all the population-level similarities and differences, there are also strong individual tendencies. In a study of half a dozen participants retelling illustrated stories to an engaged, question-asking listener, the least frequent gesturers used 5 and

Gesture. Lauren Gawne, Oxford University Press. © Lauren Gawne (2025).
DOI: 10.1093/9780198951377.003.0005

6 gestures, while the most frequent used 59 and 62 respectively for the same story (Beattie and Aboudan 1994). The two other participants used 17 and 26, which illustrates that this is not just a case of gesture use exhibiting end-extremes (all or nothing), but differences between individuals in the same interactional context. These study participants varied the number of gestures they used depending on whether they had an audience or not, but there were still high levels of variation in the number of gestures between participants across the conditions of the experiment. There are many factors that influence individual gesture preference and frequency, including autistic/allistic neurotype (McKern et al. 2023) and extroversion/introversion of personality (Li 2023).

Gesturing for an audience

The contextual nature of the variation in gesture means that the user is attending to many variables of communication when it comes to gesture use, and the audience for our communication is one major feature of that context. Gesturing 'for an audience' is about how the presence of an audience encourages certain gestural behaviour, which is different to whether the audience will actually attend to the gestures that are produced. We can think of this as how intentional the use of gesture is for an interaction; if we are conscious of how our audience is receiving information then we will change the way we gesture to best suit them.

One experimental paradigm that has been used repeatedly across almost half a century of research has been to manipulate the visibility between the person speaking and their audience. A person might be asked to retell a story to an audience that is either visible, not visible to them, or mediated by video or audio recording. People will gesture even with a non-visible audience, such as when using a telephone (Bavelas et al. 2008) or a tape-recorder (Cohen 1977). While the absence of a visible audience does not completely remove the compulsion to gesture, experiments have repeatedly shown that speakers will adapt their gestures to the context and likelihood of an audience. Cohen (1977) found that participants in a direction-giving task used a greater number of illustrative gestures when they were giving instructions face-to-face compared to when they were giving them over an audio intercom, and they used the least (but still some) when they were told they were practising alone without an audience. The face-to-face condition often involved twice as many illustrative gestures than the no-audience condition, with the intercom condition slightly above the no-audience condition. In a summary of seven earlier studies, Bavelas et al. (2008) showed that there were always more gestures in the face-to-face set up than one where the participants were visibly separated by a partition or intercom. This was true regardless of experiment set up or topic. Bavelas et al. (2008) also conducted their own study, looking at face-to-face and telephone conversations, as well as monologue audio recordings describing an image of a woman in an elaborate eighteenth-century dress. They found that people in the face-to-face context used more gestures, and that these gestures were more likely to have deictic information, interactive information, and be larger than in the telephone and recording contexts. Face-to-face participants were also less likely to encode redundant information, but more likely to provide greater information alongside speech. The interactive nature of the telephone call meant that there were still more gestures than in the recording, but for both conditions the gestures tended to be oriented towards the image, and only made so they were the size of the image. Both visibility and the presence of a live audience influenced the gesture choices of the participants in this task. This suggests that modification of gestures for an audience has several dimensions, and that we pay attention to the presence of an audience when communicating.

Gestures are therefore treated by the speaker as part of the informational content of communication. Speakers do not just modify how many gestures they make, but will modify the speech content if they know they can also make use of their gestures to be communicative. Melinger and Levelt (2004) showed that participants in an experiment who gestured while providing a description of a path between coloured dots provided fewer explicit directional words than those who gestured less, indicating that people plan the information density of their message taking into account speech and gesture. We can also tailor the usefulness of gestures depending on our relationship with our audience, beyond whether the audience is visible or not. In a study design where participants had to explain the rules of a game that involved moving around the game board, the size of participants' gestures would differ depending on whether they thought they were explaining the rules to a competitor or a collaborator (Hostetter et al. 2011). If they anticipated working with someone, gestures were generally larger, while the gestures made in explaining the rules to competitors were smaller; even though the frequency of gestures remained the same across both contexts.

Just because speakers manipulate some elements of gesture performance for their audience, this does not mean that all features of gesture performance are motivated by the audience. In a study focusing on repetition, Vajrabhaya and Pederson (2018) found that when describing a sequence of events in a video about making pizza, the size of a speakers' gestures would reduce across the three repetitions of their retelling. For example, the first time the speaker explains about stretching dough they move from the elbows, the second time the elbows are still and only the wrists move, in the final telling only the speaker's fingers move. The listeners the first and second time were two different people, so the reduction was not because the second listener was familiar with the action of stretching pizza dough. Instead Vajrabhaya and Pederson argue that the reduction was for the speaker's own conservation of motor effort, which means there is more happening than just tracking the listener's knowledge state when it comes to the use of gesture.

Gesture can provoke a response from the audience, which provides some of that dynamic context for gesture performance. Gestures can, in some contexts, take the addressee's gaze away from the speaker's face, particularly if they are low in the gesture space, or hold the speaker's turn while they search for a word (Streeck 1994). In one study, gestures that face towards the addressee when teaching origami lead to the learner collaboratively building on that gesture, while gestures that faced away from the learner were less likely to provoke the same response (Furuyama 2000). Here, gestures encouraged collaborative interaction. Gestures made while fumbling to find the right word can also open up space for the addressee to help supply the missing word (Harness Goodwin and Goodwin 1986).

The audience's response can also involve use of the same gesture features back to the speaker, which helps to demonstrate engagement with what the speaker has been saying. This can allow the speaker the chance to shape their audience's response, such as leading with a headshake to encourage a 'no' response to a question (Heath 1992). The speaker's gestures become a resource for the addressee to show that they are paying attention, by 'returning' the gesture as part of their backchannelling responses (de Fornel 1992). This also serves as a reminder that dividing the function of gesture between speaker and addressee is something of a false dichotomy, since we are all speakers and addressees across interaction.

The audience response to gesture can also be internal as well as an overt interactional response. A number of studies have demonstrated that perceiving gestures will activate the areas of the brain in the addressee that are involved in producing those actions (for an overview see Mashal et al. 2012). This activation occurs for gestures but not always for other kinds of activity, for example Holle et al. (2008) found that activation happened for iconic co-speech gestures, but not for grooming movements. Morett et al. (2020) manipulated beat gestures so that they occurred with information that was not pragmatically prominent or useful in a task where participants were required to follow instructions to click on particular shapes on a screen. These 'mis-matched' beat gestures increased the cognitive load of participants, slowing them down on the shape-clicking task, and showing that unhelpful gestures are, indeed, unhelpful in facilitating communication.

Gesturing for the speaker

Gestures are not only useful for the addressee; they also have uses relevant to the speaker as well. Many of these relate to the cognitive processing of language. We will look at different models of cognition, language, and gesture processing in Chapter 6, but here we will focus on the Lexical Retrieval Hypothesis that gesturing benefits word retrieval for speakers.

Gesture has been argued to help speakers process spatial information. Kita et al. (2017) reported on a series of experimental studies in which participants would gesture more when they were dealing with complex spatial or motion information, such as in classic 'rotation' tasks where participants have to match complex shapes that are presented from different perspectives. People will gesture even in experiments where they are alone while completing the tasks, so the gestures are not for the benefit of any audience. This spatial component to thinking means that Cook et al. (2010) were able to demonstrate that people remembered actions better if they gestured about them rather than spoke about them, and Goldin-Meadow et al. (2001) found that people who gestured while explaining their solution to a maths problem retained the answers to a memory test better. We also know that the spatial memory encoded in gestures is not always performed with an audience in mind, because Franklin (2007) has shown that people who are asked to lie about events will still 'leak' information into the gestural channel. Perhaps this is why a meta-analysis of gesture in lying found that there was a reduction in hand movements and nodding in conditions where people lie (Sporer and Schwandt 2007).

One common observation is that people are less likely to gesture when their speech is fluent, and gesture production increases during disfluent speech. The understanding has been that gesturing helps activate the mental lexicon in a way that assists word retrieval during periods of disfluency, and has come to be known as the Lexical Retrieval Hypothesis. This observation that people gesture to navigate word retrieval issues has resulted in an experimental method that has been replicated by numerous teams where gestures have been intentionally suppressed to increase the likelihood of disfluency. In the 1920s Dobrogaev (1929: 157) noted in passing that some of his collaborators had experimented with the dynamics of speech by removing people's capacity to gesture. He suggested that these results showed reduced fluency and range of vocabulary, but he did not give any specific examples. Variations on this research method have provided more detailed and quantified observations regarding the changes to people's speech in the absence of gesture, although the specifics of the method and measurements of disfluency in each publication lead to different results and conclusions. The methods of gesture suppression are varied and often novel, including false electrode plates in a chair (Rauscher et al. 1996), table-mounted buttons that the participants were asked to press continuously (Lickiss and Wellens 1978), and a 'colored garden relax-chair' that was fitted with restraints for the head, arms, legs, and feet, which participants were told was for the study of ergonomics (Rimé et al. 1984) (they are all wonderfully innovative, but Graham and Heywood's (1975) method of simply asking people to fold their hands achieves a very similar effect without the elaborate props budget). The concept of 'fluency' also varies across experiments, with some counting pauses, or reformulations, and others also taking into account speech speed, total words, and semantic complexity.

This variation in methods and outcomes makes it difficult to pin down exactly why some studies find weak or zero effects. Lickiss and Wellens (1978), for example, reported no change in verbal fluency or speech accidents in their picture matching task (Hoetjes et al. 2014 is a more recent null finding). Other issues across replications include low participant numbers (five in Graham and Heywood 1975), use of a static image task (Graham and Heywood 1975; Lickiss and Wellens 1978), the nature of the gesture constraint (active vs passive restraint), or other variables considered in each study, such as difficulty of image description in Graham and Heywood (1975).

In a series of comprehensive experiments that takes into account the various limitations of previous studies, Kısa (2022) explores and challenges the Lexical Retrieval Hypothesis. Kısa's initial replication of the restraint condition (asking people to hold down two buttons, purportedly to activate a microphone), did not find any increase in disfluencies in spatial language, which we saw above, is an area of speech where gesture is argued to play a key role in cognition, and was the main observed issue with lexical retrieval in Rauscher et al.'s (1996) influential study. In a follow up experiment, Kısa used the audience visibility experimental design with the same story retelling task, and found that people were more likely to gesture, but only when there was a visible audience. Rather than being about lexical retrieval, Kısa argued that the increase in the use of gestures during pauses has the listener-oriented function of flagging a disfluency rather than a speaker-oriented role in lexical retrieval. There are a variety of different reasons why a person might want to use gesture to signal to their audience during a disfluency; a gesture might foreshadow an impending interruption, acknowledge a current interruption the speaker intends to continue through, or signal an intention to restart the utterance. Kısa noted in this particular study that it was beat gestures that were most likely to be produced, while the Lexical Retrieval Hypothesis would suggest that more semantically-grounded gestures such as iconics would help with lexical activation. To explore this final issue in more detail, Kısa ran a third study where the use of gestures with low-probability words was explored. If a word is low-probability in a given text ('plummet' or 'swoosh', in contrast to 'are', 'can'), the speaker may be more likely to gesture with it to help the listener, or to assist their own lexical retrieval processes. In this study Kısa again found gestures were more likely to occur with the less common words, but again this only happened with a visible audience. The series of experiments in Kısa's work build a strong case that the speaker is using gesture to let their audience know they are working through the disfluency rather than helping to activate the lexicon.

Studies exploring the Lexical Retrieval Hypothesis have mostly looked at what happens when gestures are suppressed, but there are also some experiments that explore what happens when gestures are encouraged. Cravotta et al. (2019) asked their Italian-speaking participants to narrate a series of illustrated comics for a listener. Half of the participants were given no additional instructions, but half were explicitly told to gesture more. For participants who were encouraged to gesture, there were higher rates of gesture (not necessarily an assured outcome!), and the gestures made were more articulated. The participants' speech was also affected; they spoke for longer and there was more intensity in their speech. There was no change in the rate at which there were disfluencies. The traditional Lexical Retrieval Hypothesis frames gesture as 'for the speaker', but these more recent studies show that the 'for the speaker' function lets the speaker maintain control of the conversation while retrieving a word.

Acquiring gesture and language

Learning a language, whether it is a language you grow up with from childhood, or one you choose to acquire at later stages of your life, involves learning many different skills. Gesture is one of these skills that are learnt, as well as being a tool for learning other skills. In this section we start with early childhood and then adult language learning, before looking specifically at the multilingual context, and situations where new languages and communicative systems emerge. Changes in the use of gesture do not just happen at the start of our language learning journeys in childhood and adulthood. Our relationship with gesture continues to change as we age and our brains change. We will pick up the story of what happens to gesture as the brain changes in old age in the next chapter.

In this section we will move chronologically through some of the key findings about the role of gesture in development, in terms of development milestones. Ages given for these milestones should always be treated as averages; like all features of language acquisition, typical development can occur over a broad range of ages. This is particularly worth pointing out as, even more so than other fields of gesture research, language acquisition research is skewed towards English and a handful of other major languages.

Early childhood

Children's linguistic development is a gradual scaffolding of skills and competence, with gestures included in this incremental and gradual development. The earliest work on children's language development focused on spoken language milestones, including the sounds children learn to produce and the words they acquired. Bates et al. (1975) provided an important observation that intentional communication occurs before a child even uses their first words, as children make use of pointing to direct the attention of the caregivers they interact with. Once researchers turned their attention to children's gestures as well as their words, they could begin to build a richer understanding of early language acquisition.

Even before intentional gestures, there are some features of children's development that suggest a predisposition towards manual gesturing. In Masataka's (1995) study of fourteen three-month-old Japanese infants interacting with their mothers, the children showed a relationship between language-like cooing and an extension of the index finger. This relationship was not shown with non-language-like sounds like crying, or with any other handshape. This physiological tendency for the index finger to sit independent of other fingers continued in a longitudinal study from Masataka (2003), and rapidly diminished at around the age of twelve months, as intentional pointing began to be used by infants.

With the knowledge that gestural interaction precedes spoken words for hearing children, some parents have taken to using 'baby sign'. This simple form of signed communication uses individual signs (either from an existing signed language or a novel highly iconic set) and very little grammar. There is an uncomfortable irony that baby sign is promoted to hearing parents of hearing children, when so many deaf children and their families do not get the same positive message or support for using the signed modality. There is no robust evidence that the use of baby sign helps with language development (Johnston et al. 2005), although Kirk et al. (2013) did find that the use of baby sign increased the sensitivity of one set of mothers to their children's non-verbal communicative cues, a useful outcome, if not the stated intention of baby sign.

Many researchers have noted that some of the earliest actions we perform are showing and giving. These actions develop the foundations for gesture, as precursors to pointing, which is often one of the earliest gestures. Gesture is then part of the interactional skill set that children use in the process of acquiring language (see Capirci et al. 2021 for an overview). Part of the development process is the need for gross motor skills to be able to intentionally create gestures. For example, around the age of one, children become competent at tasks involving delicate gripping, which paves the way for the dexterity to perform short action gestures. Alongside pointing, children's earliest gestures are conventional gestures (such as a head shake for 'no', or holding an imaginary telephone or bottle), with iconic gestures coming later as motor skills and communicative range expand. By the time children are using their first words, they typically have a larger set of gestures, and use these more frequently than words, but by the age of two the number of words has exploded, and they are used a great deal more centrally in communication than gestures (Iverson et al. 1994).

The emergence of words does not mean gesture takes a back-seat role in acquisition. In early infant speech, gesture still plays a key role.

Rather than thinking about a jump from one word utterances ('more', 'duck', 'no') to two word utterances ('more cheese', 'give duck', 'no sleep'), there is a key point between these: a one word + one gesture combination (Clark and Kelly 2021), such as a pointing action towards the cheese on the table, or a grabbing action towards a favourite toy duck. It is an important stage in development, but not one that gets a lot of attention in baby milestone journals. Kelly (2014) has shown that one possible motivation for these word + gesture combinations is that they are more useful in getting caregiver attention than either a word or a gesture used alone. These pairs start with less synchrony and become more tightly combined over the second year of life. These word + gesture pairs are also systematic in their use and meaning; before synchronization they tend to have the same function (pointing at, and naming, an object), but, as children develop, the word adds different information, such as saying the word 'book' while presenting it to a caregiver to read. Competency with word + gesture is a sign of cognitive development that leads to the two-word stage. This developmental stage is also observed for sign + gesture combinations for children acquiring a signed language (Torigoe and Takei 2001).

Use of gesture at early milestones appears to robustly predict language development at later milestones. Rowe et al. (2021) provide a good survey of this literature. For example, the use of 'show' and 'give' gestures for a group of predominantly English-speaking children from the USA at 10 months and the use of pointing gestures at 14 months predict vocabulary use at 18 months (Choi et al. 2021). The predictive effects can be seen in syntax as well as vocabulary; use of gesture + speech combinations at one and a half years old predicted the complexity of English-speaking children's sentence production at three and a half (Rowe and Goldin-Meadow 2009). At older ages, English speaking children who tell a story at the age of five that involves a character viewpoint in gesture tell better structured stories at ages six, seven, and eight than children who do not gesture in this way (Demir et al. 2015).

Exactly what features of gesture use show a positive predictive power can vary from study to study. In one line of research the function of pointing was a predictor, with declarative pointing (requesting attention towards an object rather than an action) positively associated with language skill but imperative pointing (requesting action, such as retrieving an object) showing no such relationship (see Colonnesi et al. (2010) for a meta-analysis of twenty-five papers including with English, Italian, Spanish, and Japanese speakers). In contrast, Lüke et al. (2017) found that the function of the point was not an important factor for a group of one-year-old German-speaking children, but rather the form, with frequency of points using an extended index finger rather than full hand or palm, being a predictor of later language skills at two years, regardless of whether it was declarative or imperative in function, suggesting that the use of the index finger is an indicator of typical linguistic development in this cohort. As we better understand the relationship between gesture and language production across different age spans, and in a range of linguistic and cultural contexts, it may be that we find some general predictive tendencies, and some that are context specific.

Understanding the relationship between gesture use and general linguistic development can be an important additional perspective to provide early diagnostic and intervention options for non-typical language development. For example in Lüke et al.'s (2017) study of infant pointing above, attending to handshape use in pre-verbal infants could be a way to identify children at risk of language delay. The use of gesture as not only a diagnostic, but an intervention, had mixed results in the survey from Rowe et al. (2021: 99–100). They observed that encouraging parents to gesture more in interaction with their children does not always result in a sustained change to their behaviour, or to their children's gesturing, in studies to date. In one study that did show an effect, a researcher engaged fifteen seventeen-month-old English-speaking children in a weekly interactive pointing task for six weeks. In a follow-up, two weeks after the experiment, the children pointed more in the task and with caregivers. The children also showed increased vocabulary within the task. This suggests that the relationships between gesture use and language development is causal. When it comes to understanding why this causal relationship might exist, Rowe et al. (2021) suggest four potentially mutually reinforcing reasons. The first is that gesture reflects general skills in linguistic production and comprehension, and that the different modality shows these general skills at slightly different points in time. The second is that gestures from children encourage more and more helpful interaction from caregivers. Children have lots of different strategies to get the attention of those around them, but gestures are very salient for caregivers. The third is that gestures specifically help children to solicit information that they prioritize. Children can more readily learn the word for a thing or an action if that is what they are engaged by in the moment. The fourth and final reason is that gestures can aid children's comprehension, scaffolding understanding and reducing mapping errors.

One of the challenges of studying gesture in infants, especially gestures produced before words, is that it is difficult to ascribe intention to these gestures. Liszkowski (2008) suggests some criteria for assessing gesture intentionality, including looking to adults, persistence, and use of conventionalized forms. While it is not clear what the intention behind actions and gestures are for infants, they will often be interpreted as communicative by caregivers. Children are only one half of interaction; caregivers provide the content and context for language acquisition to occur.

Caregivers play an important and changing role in how they interact with children's earliest actions and gestures, and modify their behaviour as children's language development changes (Özçalışkan and Dimitrova 2013). While we have seen how people often include information in gestures that is not included in speech, Iverson et al. (1999) found that mothers of a dozen Italian children around the age of a year-and-a-half mostly used gestures that reinforced the message of the speech, and used fewer gestures overall. This study and others have found that mothers (who made up all caregivers in the cited studies) used mostly deictic gestures and conventional gestures like emblems (Capirci et al. 2021: 126). When children start using more iconic gestures at around twenty-six months of age, parental use of iconic gestures also increases (Özçalışkan and Dimitrova 2013). Of course, the way caregivers interact with children varies greatly across cultures, and this includes the way gesture is included in interactions. For example, in a small study comparing mother–child pairs speaking English (USA) and Mandarin (Taiwan), the Mandarin-speaking mothers were three times more likely to gesture with their children than the English-speaking mothers (Goldin-Meadow and Saltzman 2000). Children learn about things such as complex movements through the information in gestures directed towards them (Aussems and Kita 2019). We saw that children's own gestures can be predictive of later language development, but caregiver gestures are also predictive of gesture competence and later vocabulary development (Özçalışkan and Dimitrova 2013).

Later childhood

Through early childhood, the use of gesture becomes part of more complex interactions. Beaupoil-Hourdel (2021) shows how French and English children learn to use a shrug before the age of three, but at this age it is used as a simple negative. From the age of three onwards there is a shift and it becomes more complex and multifunctional, as children begin to use it to manage turn-taking and alongside speech. The frequency of the gesture does not change, but the function does.

These kind of developments of the gesture repertoire continues across childhood. As children's discourse becomes more adult-like, this includes the use of metaphoric gestures and more discourse-related gestures like beats. While the frequency of pointing gestures remains relatively stable, Mayberry and Nicoladis (2000) showed two- and three-year-old French-speaking boys increased their use of iconic and beat gestures over this period. Colletta (2004) similarly showed that frequency of use of beat gestures increases across the primary school years, as do metaphoric and abstract deictic gestures. These gestures require the ability to use complex features of language; for example beat gestures require the speaker to understand the role of emphasis in discourse, and metaphoric gestures require the speaker to have acquired culturally salient metaphors for abstract concepts such as time.

Later-childhood gesture has been studied in the educational context to understand cognitive development regarding complex tasks such as logical reasoning and mathematics. One area that has been well-studied is Jean Piaget's concept of 'conservation', which is the understanding that a quantity will remain consistent even if the shape of a container changes. Pouring water from a tall skinny glass into a wider glass will result in the water sitting lower in the wide glass as it has a wider area to cover

(Figure 11). Children do not instinctively grasp this, reasoning that the water sitting higher in the skinny glass is a result of that vessel having more water. It takes children until sometime between the age of seven and eleven to be able to understand that the quantity or volume is conserved, not altered, by the different arrangement.

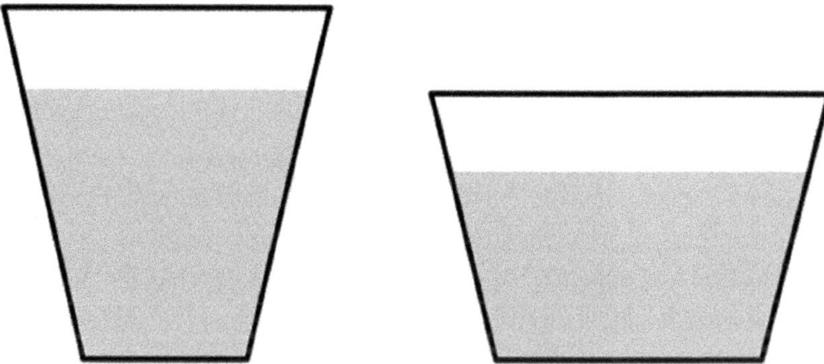

Figure 11 Demonstrating conservation of liquid in differently shaped containers

Breckinridge Church and Goldin-Meadow (1986) looked at the language and gestures that a group of five–eight-year-old English-speaking children in the USA used when explaining the relationship between different shaped vessels as part of a series of Piagetian conservation tasks, such as pouring water between different shaped vessels. They found that there was a mismatch in the information contained in the speech and gestures of some children when they were asked to explain their reasoning, either because the gesture showed different information (e.g. speech described action, gesture showed dimension), or additional information (speech talked about width of vessel, but gesture also showed depth) to their verbal reasoning. These children also showed greater inconsistency in their reasoning about different conservation tasks. In a second study, these 'mismatch' children were more receptive to training about property conservation, suggesting that the mismatched gestures and inconsistent reasoning indicated they were ready to make the developmental step for this particular form of reasoning. In a later study in the same paradigm, Goldin-Meadow and Sandhofer (1999) found that adults watching children reason about these tasks make use of the additional information in the children's gesture channel not found in the verbal channel, but would get confused if the mismatch is of different information in the verbal and gestural channel. This suggests that adults are sensitive to the information in children's gestures.

Homesign

For some children, their early language acquisition does not take a typical developmental path. Sometimes a child will grow up deaf in a spoken language household where there is no signed language used. For some children, this will be because there are no other deaf or signing people in their village or local area. For children in Western, developed countries, this is often because of still-entrenched ideologies of 'oralism', where children are denied access to an existing signed language and signing community. In situations where a child is not raised in a signing environment, a rudimentary signed system can emerge to allow the family to communicate. These are known as homesign.

Homesign was briefly introduced in Chapter 2, alongside village sign systems that might be adopted by a wider community. Homesign and other small emergent signing systems are interesting in the context of acquisition, because what fuels these systems are the gestures used in everyday interaction. The children who receive this gestural input do something very different with it than their hearing agemates who receive gestural input alongside speech. The homesign systems children innovate show more structure than the input they are given by caregivers—including more systematic ordering of elements (Goldin-Meadow et al. 1984) and the systematic structure of handshape and movement in individual signs (Goldin-Meadow and Mylander 1990). These children will use the structured communicative system they have created to interact with their caregivers, make requests, tell stories, and talk to themselves. Rather than the parents creating the structure, it is the child who develops more language-like structure from the variable and idiosyncratic raw material of caregiver gestures. Indeed, in one study, only 50 per cent of the mother's gestures fit into the stable handshape meaning model the child had created, and 25 per cent of her gestures were uninterpretable to the researchers, who note that this means they are also likely to be uninterpretable for the child as well (Goldin-Meadow and Mylander 1990: 557).

Where deaf children are given the chance to come together, they can continue to develop a linguistic system of communication, moving from homesign to a fully-fledged signed language. Village signed languages of this type that have been documented include Kata Kolok (northern Bali, Indonesia) and Al-Sayyid Bedouin Sign Language (southern Israel). The birth and development of Nicaraguan Sign Language from the formalization of education for deaf children in the country has been well-documented since the mid-1980s (Senghas et al. 2004). Examples from across homesign, village sign, and the rapid development of Nicaraguan Sign Language illustrate how children can use gestural input as the material for the development of a signed language, but that they will go on to create features of grammar that differentiate signed language from co-speech gesture, and where there is a community for the language this will continue to be refined by future generations of signers.

Gesture and multiple languages

When different languages come together in a person's repertoire, there are a variety of effects on gesture production. Most gesture research focuses on the acquisition of one specific language, or the addition of one language to a person's repertoire. This makes sense from an experiment design perspective—controlling the variables involved in the research—but does not necessarily reflect the reality that monolingualism is not the default setting for most people, across human history and in the world today. The body of research that focuses on multilingual contexts is small, but offers a number of insights about the role of gesture in communication. In this section we look at the general research on multilingual gesturers, taking into account the experiences of people who were raised in multilingual contexts, and those who acquired multiple languages across their lifespans. There is a separate section on gesture in the formal language acquisition context, as there is a specific research stream that has explored the gestures of both learners and teachers in this context.

Multilingual gesturers

Multilingual individuals are not multiple monolinguals inhabiting one brain. The multiple languages in a person's repertoire exert influence on each other, as do the social and cultural context in which each of those languages is used. As Nicoladis and Smithson's (2021) recent summary of work on gesture in bilingual language acquisition demonstrates, there is relatively little written about this topic, and there are often contradictory results in terms of frequency or function of gesture. This may be due to different cultural and linguistic contexts in which people acquire multilingual competence, or some third pressure, like a preference for using different languages in different communicative tasks.

In highly multilingual contexts, gesture may take on a heavier communicative function. Krajcik (2020) looked at the gestures that accompany placement verbs like 'put' for people in Senegal who spoke both Joola Kujireray and French, as well as between one and four other languages. Speakers used general placement verbs, but their handshape gave more information about the shape of the object and how it was being placed. This is distinct from bilingual contexts where the gestures do not necessarily show information that is not encoded in the verb semantics (e.g. Gullberg 2009).

People whose repertoire includes both spoken and signed languages show particularly interesting patterns of convergence. These cohorts, known as 'bimodal bilinguals' will use lexical signs from their signed language alongside their spoken language, particularly in contexts where both of their languages are activated (Emmorey et al. 2008a). This code-blending shows the same kind of temporal and semantic synchrony with speech that we explored for co-speech gestures in Chapter 2, but also have the formal features, like a specific handshape and place of articulation, of linguistic signs. Someone in this context signing about a bird (in this case, Tweety and Sylvester make a cameo again) would use the bird sign alongside their speech. Sometimes the co-expressed sign includes information that is not in the spoken word that co-occurs, such as when one participant used the sign for bird with the word Tweety, which provides additional information about who Tweety is (Emmorey et al. 2008a: 8). This is a code-blend, as opposed to code-switching where a person may move between languages for an audience that is also proficient in both (Lillo-Martin et al. 2016). While code-blends are more likely to occur in contexts where both languages are activated, and therefore in contexts where the audience will be more likely to know the sign, bimodal bilinguals do use these code-blends when talking to non-signers, and also use a greater variety of handshapes in their co-speech gestures overall (Casey and Emmorey 2009). Code-blending is uniquely a feature of contexts where a person has both signed and spoken languages available to them. The theory behind why bimodal bilinguals use code-blending is that it is actually more cognitive effort to stop accessing part of your linguistic repertoire, and without the physical constraint of the shared linear spoken modality, we see this coming through in the co-speech gesture stream.

Formal language learning

For language acquisition after childhood, distinguishing a second language (L2) learner from someone who is functionally bilingual is, at some point in the acquisition process, an arbitrary distinction. There is a body of work that looks specifically at the gestures of people whose language acquisition is structured around formal classroom education, as well as the gestures of those who are educating them. This work shows that learners and teachers use gesture in a range of complex ways that change across the stages of language learning. It may be tempting to think that people reach for gesture to replace missing words but research does not bear this out. People do not tend to pantomime their way through early language acquisition, but use gesture to provide additional semantic information (Brown and Gullberg 2008). Second language speakers are rated as more proficient speakers of that language when the person assessing them can see their gestures as well as hear their speech (Gullberg 1998). L2 speakers also tend to use more gestures than native speakers, although this does not necessarily mean their gestures are more informative or compensating.

One of the major areas of focus in the study of gesture and second language acquisition is the cross-linguistic influence on gesture production. We know that the languages that a person already knows can affect things like their speech accent, but gestural behaviours are also influenced by our existing repertoire.

The experimental work on path and manner motion verbs that we saw in Chapter 4 has also been conducted with people who are learning a second language, particularly where people are learning a language where the verb does something different with path and manner information than the language they already speak. Stam (2017) analysed the use of motion gestures by a Spanish speaker learning English at three intervals in a fourteen year period. While the speaker produces grammatical sentences of similar structure across this extended period, her gestures change and become more like English speakers performing the same narrative retelling task. At the first stage her gestures are very segmented with multiple different actions for each element of the motion, but nine years later she is able to package the gesture as a single event. At the final time recorded, the timing of the path gesture is not with the verb, as is the tendency for Spanish speakers, since path is encoded in the Spanish verb. Instead, her gesture is with the satellite of the verb where the path is encoded (e.g. 'up'). Her use of gesture in English is not exactly the same as the English speakers, but it is closer. On analogy with a learner's accent in their speech, this speaker's gestural 'accent' becomes less distinct over time. Stam and Tellier (2021: 342) argue that in this case the gestures show how the speaker's competence at using and thinking in the target language has changed, giving evidence of the state of the interlanguage system at different points in time.

Use of these experiments have shown that it is not just a person's L2 gestures that are affected by learning a language with a different structuring of path and manner in verbs. Brown and Gullberg (2008) replicated the motion event study with monolingual Japanese and English speakers, as well as Japanese speakers with intermediate English, half of whom lived in Japan and half in the United States of America. The bilingual participants did not use the same frequency of these manner verbs as the monolingual English speakers, but they used more than the monolingual Japanese speakers. They also used manner gestures with a path type verb (e.g. a rolling gesture with the verb 'go'). The L2 English learners did not gesture like the English speakers, but they also gestured differently in Japanese to the Japanese monolinguals, producing more manner gestures. Speakers of a second language do not always gesture the same way as people who learned that language in early childhood, but they also do not gesture like their monolingual compatriots. Gullberg (2021) draws on the theory of convergence from second language acquisition studies to explain this phenomenon; two languages will become more like each other in the repertoire of a speaker, since we do not keep multiple languages in our brain completely discrete.

When it comes to convergence, learning a signed language appears to have a particular effect on gesture in a spoken first language. Casey et al. (2012) looked at the effect of a year of learning ASL on gesture in a story retelling experiment, and found that there was greater frequency of gestures, particularly iconic gestures, and, similar to what we saw for life-long ASL/English bilinguals, those gestures used a greater variety of handshapes. The ASL users were drawing on the formal repertoire of their newly acquired language in ways that were not present in the gestures of the comparison group of French, Italian, and Spanish learners. As the authors of the paper note, learning a sign language appears to be a good way to boost the gestural processes for spoken language users.

We can also use gesture to provide evidence of some of the challenges that people have with semantic distinctions in the language they are learning. Gullberg (2009) looks at the use of placement verbs and gestures by English speakers learning Dutch in the Netherlands. Dutch has two verbs that cover the same semantic space for which English speakers have the word 'put'; the first is 'zetten' (cognate with English 'set') and 'leggen' (cognate with 'lay'). The difference has to do with the shape and orientation of the object being placed, as is somewhat apparent from the cognate semantics, 'leggen' is for objects placed horizontally, and 'zetten' is for objects placed vertically. English learners of Dutch watched a video of a person putting away objects in the process of tidying a room.

These L2 Dutch speakers did not make appropriate use of 'leggen' for horizontal placement, instead overgeneralizing 'zetten'. The gestures they made in their L2 looked very similar to those in their L1, with only around 40 per cent of their gestures indicating a vertical or horizontal placement. Their gestures show that these learners do not have a strong conceptual distinction for these two Dutch verbs, but are still very much thinking with their mono-lexeme English approach. This work also shows us that the English speakers did not make frequent use of their gestures to convey information about placement orientation to compensate for information missing in their speech.

The gestures of language instructors have also been the subject of study. In early childhood language acquisition, we saw that caregiver gestures were modified to suit the developmental stage of the child. In the classroom context, the gestures of teachers have been shown to benefit students in several ways (Stam and Tellier 2021). Teachers can use gesture to inform their students about features of the language—such as indicating elements of word meaning that are important for students to learn. Teacher gesture and facial cues have been shown to help content comprehension by students (e.g. Sueyoshi and Hardison 2005).

Teachers also use gesture when assessing the competence of students practising their speaking or reading skills, often using gestures like backchannelled nodding when things are going well, or an eyebrow raise to acknowledge a student is stuck in a moment of repair, rather than jumping in with spoken feedback too soon. Teachers also use gestures to manage a classroom, such as indicating that it is someone's turn to speak, or bringing a group back together. One of the key differences between child/caregiver and student/teacher gesture contexts is that instructors can be overtly trained how to modify their gestures as part of effective teaching. Classroom language instructors also need to be aware of their own gestural repertoire, and how their own gestures may include culture-specific emblems or uses of deictics that are not necessarily understood by their language-learning students.

Conclusion

Gesture is used by both the audience and the speaker. Speakers will modify the size and frequency of their gestures to account for whether they have an audience, and for whether that audience can see them. Audience will use features of gesture back to speakers, indicating they are receptive to the way gestures are made. Gestures have also been argued to be useful for speakers and their thought processes. Gestures have been shown to be beneficial in spatial reasoning tasks. Many studies have been done exploring the Language Retrieval Hypothesis, which proposes that gestures help speakers activate their capacity to find the right word. While these studies often show an increase in gesture during disfluency, recent experimental work suggests this is because the speaker is using these gestures to let their audience know they are working through the disfluency rather than to activate the lexicon.

Across the language learning lifespan, gestures arise before words, and are used alongside words to create more complex ways of communicating. Early use of gesture is predictive of later gestural and linguistic competence. While iconic and deictic gestures appear early in language acquisition, metaphoric and beat gesture use does not consolidate until later in childhood. Deaf children who grow up without access to a spoken language will make use of the gestures in their environment to create structure in a homesign, and if they have other deaf individuals around this can consolidate into a signed language. In later acquisition, learner gestures can show stages of linguistic development, and instructor gestures can facilitate classroom learning.

Further reading and resources

The edited volume *Gesture in Language: Development Across the Lifespan* (Morgenstern and Goldin-Meadow 2021) includes many excellent chapters that provide summaries of key work on child language from infancy to later childhood, and the use of gesture in second-language acquisition. For more on the second language learning context, McCafferty and Stam's *Gesture: Second Language Acquisition and Classroom Research* (2008) is an edited volume with a range of work.

For a more general audience, Susan Goldin-Meadow's (2023) book *Thinking with Your Hands* covers her decades-long research agenda looking at gesture in language acquisition, including homesign, and her work with language and gesture in education.

6

Gesture and cognition

So far, we have looked at how people use gesture across different cultures, conversations, and stages of language acquisition. This chapter looks at both neurological and cognitive research to explore where gesture resides in the physical brain, and how it contributes to the processes of the mind. Developments in neuroimaging in recent decades have allowed us to explore the physical topography of the brain like never before. When it comes to cognition, gesture needs to be considered in relation to the production of speech, but also in relation to other cognitive processes such as movement and spatial reasoning. Cognitive models help us to make sense of how we produce multimodal communication, and neurological insights help us to understand where in the brain these processes take place. Neurology and cognition therefore represent two distinct but interdependent perspectives on the role of gesture in human communication.

In this chapter we look at work that studies the role of gesture in communication for typical populations, as well as for people in atypical populations, such as those with speech disorders or acquired brain injuries. There is a long history of using the language production of atypical populations to contrast and extrapolate normative behaviour. It is always good to remember, however, that there is sufficient variation and a great deal that we do not know even for typical populations when it comes to the brain and gesture.

Gesture. Lauren Gawne, Oxford University Press. © Lauren Gawne (2025).
DOI: 10.1093/9780198951377.003.0006

Gesture and the brain

Fay Parrill (2020) teaches cognitive science using the insights she has learnt from cognitive science, including the fact that the human mind lives inside a body and we learn better when learning is active and embodied, including through the use of gesture. Parrill has developed a process for teaching about the brain that uses the hands as a gestural model. It is a highly simplified model, but conveniently we generally tend to have a pair to hand. Make two loose fists with your thumbs tucked inside, and bring your hands together so that the base of the palm and the fingernails touch. The pinky fingers should be pointing outward, and represent the front of the brain. The fingers do a very crude job of illustrating how the brain packs in a lot of neural connections thanks to the large surface area created by the ridges. Each ridge is called a gyrus, and the groove is a sulcus, although there are far more of them in the brain than we have fingers. This is our model brain, which you can examine at any point in this chapter.

Before we begin to look at our model brain in any detail, it is worth stating very clearly that there is not a single, specific part of the brain that we can point to and label 'gesture'. The brain is a complex organ, and the production and comprehension of language, including gesture, is a series of complex skills rather than a single activity. A further complicating factor is that features of neurology are often discussed at a population level; at the individual level there is variation in the organization of the brain. I will occasionally point out some of this variation, both common and remarkable.

Brains, gesture, and bodies

Gesture has a close relationship to language in the brain, but it is also a physical activity, and as such, it is worth understanding how the brain makes the body move before we understand how those movements relate to communicative meaning.

Returning to our hand brain model, our two fists represent the two hemispheres of the brain, the left hand is the left hemisphere and the right hand is the right hemisphere. There is a big crevasse down the middle of the brain and each side is distinct and has distinct functions. In terms of general motor control, the left brain is responsible for the movement and sensation of the right half of the body, while the right brain is responsible for the left. So when you are moving your right hand to touch the left fist of your hand brain, it is your left hemisphere that is coordinating that action.

The cognitive planning of movement is done in the motor cortex, a large region that runs down the right index finger of your brain model all the way to the lowest knuckle at the base of your finger. Within this region different sections have been shown to control different parts of your body, not necessarily to the level of correspondence with individual muscles, but certainly in a way that broadly maps out the human body. The bits that control the feet and legs are tucked in at the top of the brain/finger between your second and third index knuckle. Moving down the finger moves up the body, through the torso, arm, hand, fingers, and then along the back of the hand to the face. Below that is some dedicated neural space for what is happening in the mouth and throat. There is a rather crude-looking diagram that simplifies and summarizes this mapping of the physical body onto the respective regions of the motor cortex, known as a cortical motor homunculus (Figure 12). If you don't have a hand, that region of the brain will be redistributed to the parts of the body that take on the same functions, even if they are not right next to it (Hahamy et al. 2017), so someone who uses their foot to eat, paint, and gesture will have that space dedicated to their foot instead. The motor cortex communicates with the muscles in the body through electrical signals in the nervous system, largely coordinated through the basal ganglia, which sit somewhere around your thumbnails, tucked right in below the cortex.

The body map for sensory information coming into the brain from different parts of the body has a similar arrangement, and similar prioritization of the face and hands, but runs along the middle finger rather than the index. There is a similar diagram of the cortex for sensory input, known as a cortical sensory homunculus. The separation of the motor and sensory cortex happened around 100 million years ago in placental mammals, when they diverged from marsupials (Kaas 2004).

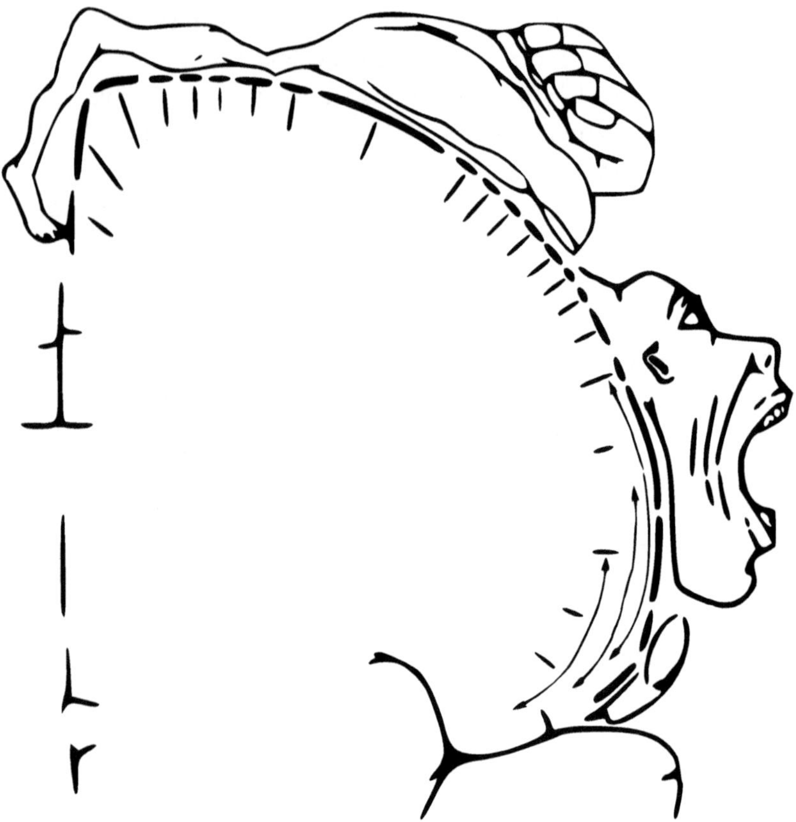

Figure 12 A cortical motor homunculus
Image by mailto:ralf@ark.in-berlin.de via Wikimedia CC A-SA 4.0 license (https://commons.
wikimedia.org/wiki/File:Motor_homunculus.svg)

One advantage of the motor cortex homunculus is that it makes visible just how much neurological real estate we dedicate to our hands, faces, and tongues. You can see the difference in the amount of brain space given to the wrists, hands, and each individual finger in contrast to the feet and toes. We move our hands and faces with incredible precision, and are highly sensitive to communicative movements made by others.

We will look at some of the evolutionary reasons the brain dedicates so much neural real estate to hands in the next chapter. The proximity of hands and faces in the cortical map also reflects observations that the coordination of the hand and mouth is one of the earliest integrations of sensorimotor systems for humans in the early months of life (Rochat 1993). This starts as a soothing reflex, indeed before babies are born they can be seen in ultrasound images bringing their hand to the mouth. There is also the Babkin Reflex, where an infant's mouth will open if their palm is pressed, which suggests a close sensorimotor linking. Before the age of six months, hands also bring objects to the mouth to explore sensory properties. We see this link continue; in one study, four-year-olds were more likely to protrude their tongue out of their mouth when engaged in motor tasks (Forrester and Rodriguez 2015). This early-life integration may have played a role in the integration of hands with speech, but this alone is not enough to explain how both hands and mouths come together in human language (Vainio 2019).

While we have been mostly focusing on the relationship between movements of the hands and mouth as part of a foundation for a multi-modal language system, we can also think about the neural relationship between gestures and other kinds of movements, such as those that we make when using tools. Tool use, like gesture, involves fine control of movement, and also involves an understanding of the properties of the tool and the aims of using it. For example, using a wooden spoon to stir a pot of soup requires the user to understand the weight of the spoon, and how much force they will need to move the spoon through the soup at the right speed to move the contents of the pot around to distribute the heat and encourage even cooking. This knowledge appears to be located in the same left motor cortex region as the area for gestures, and indicates that humans' unusually sophisticated tool use and co-speech gesture use may have evolved together as part of the same neurological skill set (Frey 2008).

This system of movement and gesture may have been given a boost by the presence of mirror neurons, which have implications for the performance and observation of action and gesture. Mirror neurons activate when a person performs an action, or watches someone perform that action, thereby 'mirroring' the neural activity without mirroring the performance of the action. Individual mirror neurons have been documented in macaque monkeys, where sensors have been placed directly onto the brain. In humans, less-precise (and less-invasive) neural imaging has been used to show activation of 'mirror systems' for specific actions. Teasing out the dimensions of what counts as performing 'similar actions' has been a major topic of research since mirror neurons were first described in macaques in the early 1990s; there is activation if a person observes a human, monkey, or dog biting, and activation if only a human is observed moving the mouth in speech-like ways (a monkey or dog moving its mouth in a similar way will not activate the mirror neurons). It is unlikely that this is exclusively a way to acquire gesture, since there is greater activation if the action being observed is already in your own repertoire. Mirror neurons may activate while watching actions, but it is also worth remembering that other parts of the brain are also required to understand the action. Therefore, mirror neurons may reinforce learning, but they are unlikely to provide the full explanation of how humans pay attention to, and learn, gestures and other actions (Arbib 2013).

Brains, gesture, and language

Now we know movement and sensation of hands and mouths are given a lot of space in the motor cortex, and that the regions that manage each are closely collocated. This does not necessarily mean that they are closely related in their function. In this section we will look at how hands and mouths come together in the task of human language.

Throughout this book, we have seen examples of how gesture and speech are not only produced together, but produced in a way that demonstrates they are tightly integrated in their planning and production. Therefore, it is worth visiting the parts of the brain that relate to language, to examine what we have learnt about gesture from studying these brain regions.

As noted above, the left and right hemispheres of the brain are responsible for movement in the opposite side of the body (the technical term for this is 'contralateralization'). Each hemisphere of the brain also specializes for other cognitive tasks. The right hemisphere is usually responsible for tasks such as facial recognition, musical processing, and spatial tasks, while the left is responsible for analytical tasks such as language and arithmetic. In some people this lateralization function is reversed, but it seems to operate as a population-level generalization. Within the left hemisphere, there are regions that are particularly relevant to the production and processing of language. The two most well-known linguistic areas of the brain are Broca's area and Wernicke's area (Figure 13).

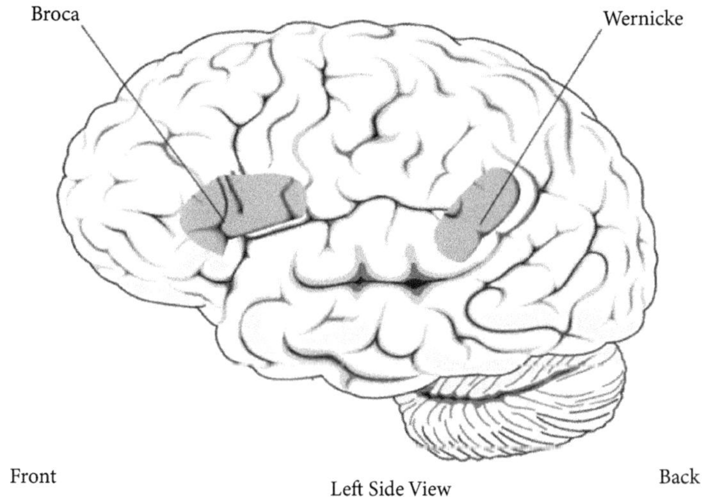

Figure 13 The brain with Broca's and Wernicke's area

Image by UX Stalin via Wikimedia CC BY-SA 4.0 license (https://commons.wikimedia.org/wiki/File:BrocasAreaSmall.png)

Broca's area is towards the front of the left lobe of the brain in the inferior frontal gyrus, somewhere above the outer edge of your eye, or around the lowest knuckle of your ring finger in our hand model. Broca's area has a role in the production of complex linguistic structures. Wernicke's area is further back along the left side of the skull in the superior temporal gyrus, past the ear, around the right side of the lowest middle-finger knuckle on the hand model (give it a prod!). Wernicke's area is associated with comprehension and content of speech. Both of these areas are named for the nineteenth-century medical men who noted commonalities in language disorders for patients with brain injuries. Broca made note of cases where people could comprehend speech but their vocabulary had been reduced to a small number of words, while Wernicke observed patients who could talk fluid nonsense but did not appear to comprehend what was said to them. Autopsies on the people they observed demonstrated damage to different parts of the brain consistent with either area. The link between speech production and Broca's area, and speech reception and Wernicke's area has been strengthened and refined using modern brain imaging techniques. There are other areas of the brain that have been shown to play a role in the processing of meaning, such as the medial temporal gyrus that runs along the back of your left hand in the fist model of the brain. The medial temporal gyrus is also used in processes including facial recognition and reading.

While these areas of the brain are often discussed for their role in language, in reality they are involved in a wider range of functions. Broca's area is also activated when performing movements of the hands and arms for specific goals, such as pinching (Nishitani and Hari 2000), and mirror neurons in Broca's area also fire while watching someone else pinching. Returning to language, both Broca's and Wernicke's areas are activated for gestural emblems, like a thumbs up, the same as for words (Xu et al. 2009), and the inferior frontal gyrus, which contains Broca's area, is implicated in the processing of iconic gestures that represent physical objects and events (Özyürek 2014). These insights from Gesture Studies expand our understanding of the role of these parts of the brain, suggesting that it is not really words that are being encoded, but some sort of 'modality-independent semiotic system' (Xu et al. 2009: 20,664). Not only do these brain regions process speech and gesture, they integrate them, and very early in cognitive processing. Integration occurs around 200–300 milliseconds from input (Kelly 2017: 247), which is the earliest time window for the brain to start processing and responding to semantic input.

An expanded understanding of the language regions of the brain allows us to consider the way gesture use may vary from the perspective of neurodiversity. Gesture has been used as a tool in autism diagnosis, with absent or infrequent gestures treated as diagnostic indicators of this neurodevelopmental type. As McKern et al. (2023) note in a systematic literature review of twenty-five studies that examined the gestures of autistic and allistic people, the data tell a more complex story. In their meta-analysis, autistic people produce fewer overall gestures, and specifically fewer deictic and emblem gestures, but results for iconic gestures were far more mixed. McKern et al. noted that the size of the effect was influenced by what the experimental task involved, and whether participants were interacting with someone they were familiar with. For example, autistic people were less likely to use deictic and iconic gestures with an unfamiliar observer (2023: 734), and more likely to use iconic gestures in unstructured tasks. This suggests the experimental paradigms might not be capturing the full picture of gesture use for neurodiverse people. Understanding not only the frequency, but also the communicative role of gesture, can help us better understand the role of gesture in the communicative styles of a range of neurotypes.

Stefanini et al. (2008) looked at the speech and gesture of young children with Down syndrome (three–eight-year-olds) who were matched with children the same age, and with another cohort that were the same developmental age. Down syndrome is a genetic condition that affects language production more than spatial and motoric cognition. The children were asked to describe pictures of objects and actions. The children with Down syndrome were more likely to use gestures than either of the other groups, and where these gestures were iconic, they were often closer to the target than spoken answers offered. This study indicates that the cohort of children with Down syndrome use their gestural skills to compensate when cognition outstrips linguistic ability.

In Chapter 5 we looked at how children develop gestural competence as part of the language learning process, and how this process continues across childhood. At the other end of the human lifespan, the brain undergoes observable changes, with brain volume decreasing, particularly in the prefrontal cortex (Scahill et al. 2003). This can affect high-level processes in this part of the brain, including language processing (Andres and Van der Linden 2000), however it is also worth attending to the fairly impressive evidence that even with these changes in the brain as we age, linguistic systems are maintained as well as they are by the dynamic network of neurons (Shafto and Tyler 2014). Ageing therefore presents us with another opportunity to consider the relationship between gesture and language in the brain. If gesture is a part of the linguistic system, we might expect that any decline in linguistic competence with age would be paralleled with a decline in gesture use. If gesture is supplemental, then we might see it being used to compensate for decline in the linguistic system. The evidence to support either hypothesis is mixed, at best. Some studies show a decrease in iconic gesture production, but not beat gesture production, with age, although this can depend on whether the iconic information being recalled is visual (the layout of a bedroom) or motoric (performing a common task). Other studies show that differences in gesture are perhaps the result of different speech styles, with older speakers using more circumlocution, perhaps to work around a reduction in mental imagery that results in fewer iconic gestures (see Göksun et al. 2021 for a more detailed summary of all of this work).

Looking at what happens to the brain when it is subjected to injury or illness provides insight into the larger questions about how linguistic and gestural systems relate and work together in communication. We have several decades of research on the effect of aphasia on gesture production. One study compared the retelling of an animated narrative and found that the participants with Broca's aphasia told the story and used gesture at the same key points as other participants (such as a downward gesture to indicate the downward movement of an object), but the co-timing and semantic integration of the narrative were reduced for the participants with aphasia (Pedelty 1987). More recent work has argued more strongly that gesture production degrades alongside speech in aphasia (Mol et al. 2013), although in one study, people with aphasia gesture more informatively than people with Alzheimer's and the general population. Goodwin's detailed, long-term, and sensitive analysis of his own father's communication as someone with aphasia demonstrates how gesture can be utilized to compensate for the verbal channel, but it is still constrained (Goodwin 2000, 2007). One study with signers illustrates that there are some elements of gesture that are less integrated into the neurolinguistic system. Facial expressions in signed languages can take on a grammatical function, for example raised eyebrows might encode an interrogative in question asking. In a series of studies, Poizner et al. (2000) showed that these grammatical facial expressions were affected in signers with Broca's aphasia, while expressive facial movements that signify emotion were not affected.

As well as these forms of aphasia that are located in specific regions of the brain, often from some kind of acute trauma, there is primary progressive aphasia, which involves the slow impairment of the whole left hemisphere, sometimes but not always as a result of a neurological condition such as Alzheimer's disease. In the speech of people with primary progressive aphasia, some gestures such as iconics can compensate for speech difficulty (Hadar 1989) and may help with lexical retrieval (Kroenke et al. 2013). As Göksun et al. (2021: 282) note in their survey of the effects of neurodegenerative disorders that affect language and gesture production, there is very little research in this area, even for diseases that affect people in larger numbers, including Parkinson's disease, Alzheimer's disease, and primary progressive aphasia.

Research in this area has the potential to provide benefits for how we diagnose neurological conditions and provide therapy. For example, one study on gesture production during a picture description task noted that people with temporo-medial mild cognitive impairment, which is characterized by a memory deficit, used more iconic gestures than a control and a group with mild Alzheimer's, especially for word retrieval and word replacement (Geladó et al. 2022). This task could potentially be used as a non-invasive tool to diagnose and actively monitor this type of cognitive impairment. Gesture can also be used as a therapy tool. We know people with aphasia can spontaneously gesture, and that these gestures can be used to compensate for lexical items. There is good reason to encourage gesture in speech therapy, and developing more tools to better utilize gesture in speech therapy for people with aphasia (Rose 2006, 2013). Finally, a better understanding of the role of gesture and other non-verbal cues in the communicative repertoire of people with neurological conditions can help in educating carers on communication differences, and facilitate better communication in contexts where gesture can carry a more significant communicative load (Seidl et al. 2012). Multiple-Modality Aphasia Treatment (M-MAT) is one example of a model that considers the valuable contribution gesture can make to communication for people with aphasia (Clough and Duff 2020).

Gesture and the mind

It is one thing to know where in the physical space of the brain gesture is being produced, it is another thing to have a coherent and consistent model of how gesture works alongside other parts of language in human communication. Cognitive models allow us to abstract away from specific brain regions, to think about an ordered series of processes that take us from the initial conceptualization of an idea to the production of a multimodal utterance that includes both speech and gesture. Cognitive models allow us to consider the 'mind' in the abstract, rather than the 'brain' as a physical organ. They also allow us to consider the many steps, processes and skills required for the complex phenomenon we refer to as 'language', and where gesture sits amongst those skills and processes.

Psychologists and linguists in the field of cognitive linguistics have participated in a long and sustained debate about the role of gesture in language production. Different models have potentially different implications for our understanding of language, and can lead to different interpretations of the importance of gesture in cognition and communication. The earliest models were mostly motivated by behavioural evidence—how people used gesture—but increasingly cognitive models also make use of the kind of neurological information we discussed above. Models have the benefit of being generalizations, which smooths out some of the variation we see in individual neurology.

There are many models of speech production that do not include gesture, but gesture models must contend with speech. In this section we start with a classic language model that has been built on by gesture researchers. Next, we consider some key models that look at how gesture is incorporated into language production, and the evidence that motivates them. Finally, we investigate models that explore features of gesture use beyond its integration with speech. For each of these models, the focus is on key features, and points of difference with other models. Different models draw on different evidence, and highlight different observations about gesture and how it relates to language, movement, and cognition. The path forward is very unlikely to be one of convergence into a single, unified model of gesture in cognitive processing, but a richer understanding that different uses of gesture have different cognitive underpinnings.

Levelt's (1989) model of speech production

Cognitive models of speech production must account for how we move from abstract ideas through to physically producing speech. Not only do we have to decide what to communicate, but we need to plan how to communicate thought (which does not have to be linear) into speech (which is linear), produced word-by-word, sound-by-sound, or sign-by-sign, one unit at a time. Levelt's (1989) work focused on languages that use the vocal modality. While Levelt's model did not include gesture, it has been used as the starting point for much of the conversation about how gesture fits into language production. This model has been praised for its comprehensiveness and theoretical coherence and it continues to be developed, critiqued and refined. Levelt's original model was laid out in a book-length treatment, detailing the process from the conceptualization of thought to the physical articulation of speech. Thinking of language as a set of different processes opens up the possibility that utterance planning can be serial, involving parallel processes, self-checks, and feedback mechanisms.

Figure 14 is an extremely simplified form of Levelt's original model. Broadly put, as we move from a 'conceptualizer' to a 'formulator' to an 'articulator', each step is monitored and refined through feedback mechanisms.

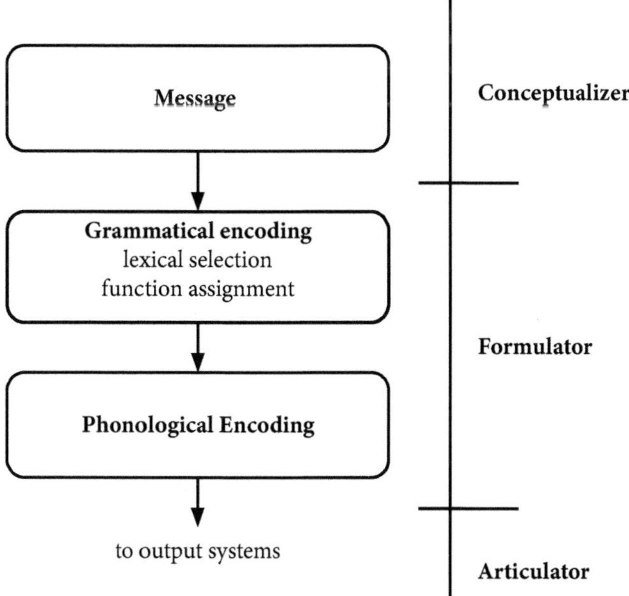

Figure 14 A simplified form of Levelt's model of speech production

The models that build on this to account for gesture production all take as a starting point that speech and gesture are tightly integrated in human communication. They add an additional set of gesture production processes that parallel the speech processes to consider how gesture might fit with Levelt's model of language production.

Models of gesture and speech production

Language production models that include gesture share the observation that gesture is functionally and temporally aligned with speech, evidence of which we covered in Chapter 2. In this section we will look at two key models of gesture and speech production; the Sketch Model and the Interface Model, both of which build on Levelt's model. We also look at McNeill's Growth Point Model as an example of a gesture and speech production model that does not take Levelt's work as its starting point.

Sketch Model

de Ruiter (2000) expands Levelt's speech production model to examine how gesture might fit within it. In this model, the conceptualizer includes both speech and gesture; there is a preverbal message for speech and a spatiotemporal sketch for gesture. The addition of this sketch feature, which focuses on what gesture contributes to the communication, gives this model its name. From here speech and gesture diverge into a speech formulator and a gesture generator, where a motor programme is developed for each in their respective channels. In this model, gesture and speech are closely planned at the conceptualization stage, stemming from the same communicative intent, but they are separate and parallel in how they are produced. de Ruiter has continued to refine the model, in a 2017 formulation he emphasizes that the modalities are asymmetric in their importance, with speech the dominant modality, and that gestures that contribute semantic content (e.g. iconic gestures) are mostly redundant when they co-occur with speech. This updated version is the Asymmetric Redundancy Sketch Model (de Ruiter et al. 2017). Figure 15 is a very simplified version of the Sketch Model that emphasizes the dual strands of processing.

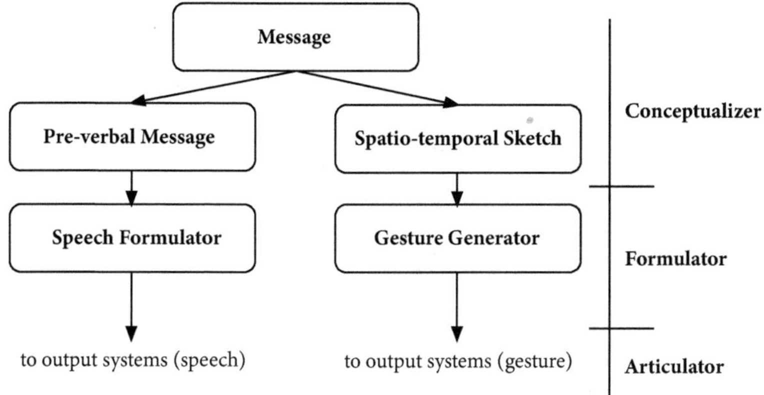

Figure 15 A simplified form of the Sketch Model

Interface Model

This model from Kita and Özyürck (2003) is also based on Levelt's speech production model. In this model, there is more emphasis placed on the conceptualizer in selecting the modality of expression. From there, the formulator includes both an action generator and a message generator, but most importantly in this model, these two components of the model are not separate parallel processors, but they interact. This element of the model is important for Kita and Özyürek as it explains the way that verb structure in a language influences the structure of gesture. It is this interface of the two parallel processes (Figure 16) that gives this model its name. Returning to their work on motion verbs, the message generator is responsible for encoding an action (rolling down the hill), in which path or manner may be more central depending on the language, and this will influence the shape of the gesture being put together in the gesture generator.

Growth Point

Not all multimodal models of language production take Levelt's work as a starting point. One early and influential model was put forward by McNeill (1992, 2005). McNeill was developing his theory of gesture production around the same time Levelt published his model. In McNeill's work, gesture and speech are conceptualized together in a pre-linguistic

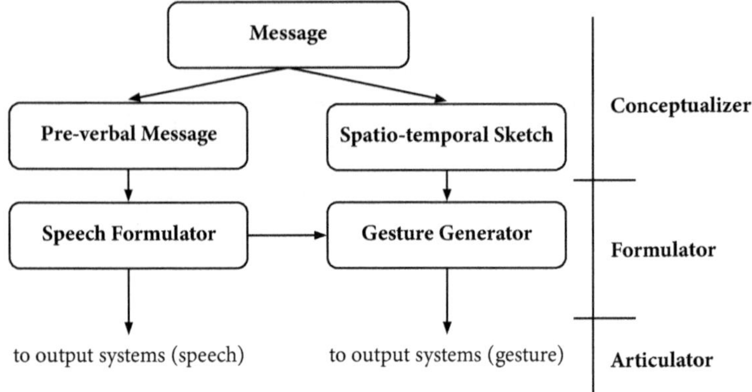

Figure 16 A simplified form of the Interface Model

stage of thought known as the 'growth point'. From there, the conceptualizer shapes the communicative intent and the formulator turns this intention into speech (Figure 17). Gesture is seen by McNeill as a direct window into thought. In this model gesture is less structurally complex and less conventionalized than speech, because it does not pass through the same kind of formulators that give the speech stream its linguistic structure. This feature of the model is why de Ruiter (2007) refers to a highly summarized form of McNeill's work as a 'window architecture' model, although you will find the term 'growth point' more commonly in the gesture literature.

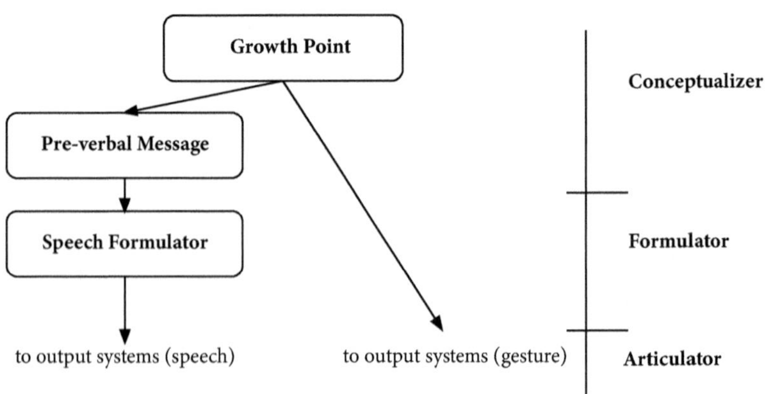

Figure 17 A simplified form of the Growth Point Model

The implication of this model is that gesture is showing us features of thought that are unconstrained by linguistic structuring. A great deal of work has been done since the publication of McNeill's early work that focuses on the communicative intent of gesture, such as the work that influenced the Interface Model, and studies in the previous chapter that show people modify gesture behaviours depending on whether they are visible to the audience. This work has provided counter-evidence that gesture is not just a simple 'window' into thought. Still, this early model has been very influential for our understanding of the processing of gesture and speech.

Models of gesture in general cognition

As we saw above, gesture is neurologically integrated into our larger movement systems. Some cognitive models have attempted to make sense of this relationship rather than focusing specifically on the relationship between language and gesture. These models consider how gesture is integrated into spatial thought processes, and how these may be subsequently linked to language production. Such models fit into a larger trend of thinking about 'embodied cognition', and how human thought cannot be separated from the fact that we exist in bodies in physical reality. We have touched on embodied cognition when looking at spatial metaphors for time in Chapter 4, but embodied cognition is much broader. Here we look at two key models that have been proposed.

Gesture as Simulated Action

The Gesture as Simulated Action model, proposed by Hostetter and Alibali (2008, 2019), argues that representational gestures, such as iconics, are generated by communicating about actions. The embodied nature of language means that when we use language to talk about actions, we are still activating the motor processing parts of the brain, and this spills over into gestures that accompany speech.

This model can be seen as something of one single component of a larger model of language production—models that are built on Levelt's work go from conceptualization all the way through to production— and this model of gesture as simulated action proposes a very detailed account of a very particular kind of gesture, one which can be related to other kinds of movement. Hostetter and Alibali (2008: 503) acknowledge that all of language is not necessarily based on simulated action, so the gesture as simulated action model only accounts for a particular set of actions. The authors draw on both the link between motor actions and gesture that we saw in the first half of this chapter, and production evidence. For example, a person is more likely to gesture when describing a pattern of dots if they had to previously trace out the triangle shape that those dots were in, rather than just previously seeing the triangle drawn out as lines between the dots.

Gesture for Conceptualization

The Gesture for Conceptualization model proposed by Kita et al. (2017) looks at a number of ways gesture influences different human thought processes. Central to this model is the premise that gesture is 'schematic' in nature; detail is stripped away, and only key features of shape or movement are retained. Drawing on a range of research from their own team and others, the authors point to four ways that gesture helps with conceptualization. First, gesture is involved in the activation of spatial thought, as evidenced by studies where people completing tasks of mentally rotating abstract shapes do better if given the opportunity to gesture. Second, gesture helps manipulate spatial information, so those people who use gesture in a mental rotation task and then asked to stop will still perform better at the next non-gesturing trial than those who never got the opportunity to gesture. Third, gesture can package information, we have seen tasks where the structure of the verb in a language influences the nature of the gesture, but asking people to make a particular kind of gesture in English can change how many sentences they will break an action up into while reporting; a single gesture encourages a single verb, a different path and manner gesture encourages two sentences. Finally, gestures help explore thought, which we saw in the previous chapter with children whose gestures are mismatched to their explanation of a spatial reasoning task. One of the advantages of this model is that it positions the lack of complexity in gesture as a cognitive advantage for complex thought, rather than as a reduction in detail.

Table 3 provides a summary of the cognitive models introduced above. These accounts of seemingly incongruous models might not actually be so incompatible if we consider there is not one single role that gesture has within communication. As Wagner Cook (2021) notes, gesture appears to be used in cognition at a number of levels; it can be used for thinking that underpins communication regardless of modality, it can be used as part of the conceptualization and formalization of language production at multiple levels of linguistic structure, and it can be used in more general cognitive processes that relate to communication, including working memory, visual memory, and motor memory. There are also ways these models can be enriched with the inclusion of more linguistic diversity, especially with regard to the gestures that are used with signed languages.

Table 3 Summary of the different models of gesture production

Model type	Model name	Summary	Reference
Gesture and language production	Sketch Model	Conceputalizer includes a preverbal message for speech and a spatiotemporal sketch for gesture	de Ruiter (2000), de Ruiter et al. (2017)
	Interface Model	The language formulator influences the gesture formulator to shape the structure of gesture	Kita and Özyürek (2003)
	Growth Point Model	Gesture and speech conceptualized together but gesture is not constrained by speech	McNeill (1992, 2005)
Gesture, action, and thought	Gesture as Simulated Action	Spatial and action features of language activate motor function and spill over into gesture	Hostetter and Alibali (2008, 2019)
	Gesture for conceptualization	Schematic nature of gesture is used in conceptualization of action and language	Kita et al. (2017)

Models of gesture perception

The models above all look at how gesture and speech are produced together. Just as there is less work on gesture comprehension, there are fewer models that seek to represent speech and gesture perception.

A good summary of the neurological and behavioural evidence we have for how gesture perception integrates into speech perception is provided by Kelly (2017). Gesture perception is integrated closely with speech perception in three key ways, which all relate to evidence we have seen in earlier chapters. Gesture is integrated into pragmatic comprehension, through negotiation turn-taking and back-channelling. Gesture perception is also closely related to concrete semantics, such as spatial information, however it is worth noting that it does not appear to be implicated in the processing of abstract semantic information. Abstract semantic concepts like ideas, principles, or laws become relevant to the gesture system only when mapped onto more concrete features, through the process of metaphoric gestures. Gesture processing appears to use similar resources to other image-based processing including photographs (Wu and Coulson 2011). Finally, gesture comprehension is closely related to suprasegmental phonetic processes such as stress and intonation, which is how we can shift people's perception of word stress though changing the downstroke of a beat gesture. Although gesture is linked to this higher-level phonological processing, there is very little evidence that gesture is closely integrated into segmental phonetics (the level of individual sounds). As with production models, understanding the role of gesture in perception and processing models helps us further refine the relationship between speech and other parts of language. Here, gesture appears critical to the embodied elements of language, but less directly related to the more abstract, structural features of the speech stream.

Conclusion

We need to understand gesture both with regard to where it is located in the physical brain, and how it is part of cognitive processes in the mind. Gesture is part of the sensorimotor system, a system which gives a lot of neural activity to actions and sensations of the hands, arms, and face. There is a strong motor link between the hands and the mouth, as seen in human development. Gesture is also closely linked with language in the brain, activating many of the same regions, including Broca's and Wernicke's areas. Gesture has also been shown to suffer similar impairment to language for people with acquired brain injuries. A better understanding of how gesture and language change with age, and age-acquired brain changes, can help to provide insights into and resources for how we approach diseases including Parkinson's disease, Alzheimer's disease, and primary progressive aphasia.

Cognitive models allow us to consider the evidence from language and gesture production to build an understanding of the sequence of steps required to move from the abstract processes of thought to the concrete production of speech and gesture. There are different models of language and gesture production, including the Sketch Model, Interface Model, and Growth Point Model. There are also models for understanding the relationship between gesture, movement, and thought, including Gesture as Simulated Action and Gesture For Conceptualization. There are also models of gesture perception and processing, which shows that there are some features of language that gesture is more closely associated with than others.

Further reading and resources

Clough and Duff (2020) provide a summary of work on using gesture with people who have neurogenic communication disorders (including from acquired brain injury and Alzheimer's) and also provide a detailed and citation-rich summary on the communicative role of gesture and the different cognitive models that have been proposed for multimodal language production. de Ruiter (2007) is a classic chapter that summarizes the key work done on cognitive models of language processing and examines the implications of some key models.

7

The past and future

So far, we have been focusing on the ways that gesture is an integrated part of a multimodal system of human communication. When we look back towards the origins of human language, there is an ongoing debate about the role of gesture in the rise of our current skill set. This chapter summarizes key positions within the debate on the role of gesture in language evolution. We start with a brief outline of this debate, before taking a pause to consider the evidence for gesture-like behaviour in other animals. We will appraise the behaviour of those primates that we are close to in the tree of life, as well as those animals that are close to us socially through domestication. We then draw on this evidence, as well as cognitive, neurological, and communicative evidence discussed in earlier chapters, to look at some of the main arguments in the debate about the role of gesture in the development of modern human language.

Once we have looked backwards to see where we have come from, we turn to consider the future of human gesture. We look at how Gesture Studies is informing the way we communicate with digital devices, and how those devices and avatars are gesturing to us in return. Finally, we look at the ways we continue to gesture to each other in digital formats, and how online communication is returning to centring gesture as part of human communication.

Debates about the origin of language

There are two histories to tell when looking at the place of gesture in language evolution. The first is the long, deep history of how humans

Gesture. Lauren Gawne, Oxford University Press. © Lauren Gawne (2025).
DOI: 10.1093/9780198951377.003.0007

evolved, and particularly how we evolved to speak and gesture as we do. The second history we have to tell is the history of how gesture has been theorized to have played a role in this evolution. As will hopefully become clear in this chapter, everything we can say about the first history is speculation based on secondary evidence. For this reason, let's start with the documented history of how humans have speculated about the origins of language.

The nineteenth-century work on the theory of evolution included fervent discussion of human evolution, and the origins of our capacity for language. There were any number of theories about how language might have begun, including, but not limited to, that it originated in song, in the development of ritual and religion, in the mimicry of the environment, in the replacement of grooming with gossip, or in a pre-existing capacity for gesture. This last theory is of particular interest to us.

At this time, the debates were so speculative, and so unlikely to be sufficiently evidenced, that the Société de Linguistique de Paris banned all contributions on the topic of the origin of language in 1865, and the Philological Society of London followed suit in 1873. The discussion has been reanimated in the last few decades, thanks to advances in the fields of genetics, neurology, and psychology as well as advances in our understanding of the world's linguistic diversity, and the way other species communicate. We also have a better understanding of the fact that when we talk about 'language' we actually mean a whole host of skills, including symbolic thinking, fine motor skills, joint attention, and a better understanding of gesture and its role in human and non-human communication. Equipped with this knowledge we have a better opportunity than the nineteenth-century philologists to develop an understanding of the nature of human language evolution.

We can broadly categorize theories of language evolution in two groups. The first group of theories propose that language is so complex that the only explanation for it is that it arose from existing pre-linguistic systems. These are known as continuity theories. The second group of theories argues that language is so complex, and so unique in the animal kingdom, that the only explanation for it is that it arose suddenly and all at once. These are known as discontinuity theories. Theories of both types draw on evidence of how gesture is used in animals beyond humans. Therefore, before we visit these theories about the origins of human language, we will look at gesture and gesture-like behaviour in primates and other animals.

Gesture and other species

To understand how gesture contributes to debates about the origin of human language, it is worth considering whether the capacity to gesture is something that is uniquely human. We can look at the evidence for gesture, or gesture-like behaviour, in other animals. Looking for evidence in different species—both those closely related to us and those not so closely related to us—lets us better understand which elements of this skill set are from common ancestors and which can arise across animal families. When it comes to species closer to humans, we will look at the communicative skills of other members of the great ape group, including chimpanzees, bonobos, and gorillas. In this chapter we are going to distinguish very carefully between two different types of reported evidence when it comes to apes and gesture. The first is the use of signed language as a modality in an attempt by humans to instruct and communicate with specific individuals in a species, the second is a documented capacity for gesture-like communication in groups of apes in their own social environment. Then we will turn to the evidence for gesture use in animals beyond primates.

Researchers who study the gestural communication of other species are very clear to point out that these 'gesture' systems are not exactly the same as human gesture, but need to be studied on their own terms (Tomasello and Call 2019; Hobaiter 2020). The most immediately obvious distinction is that other animals do not have linguistic structures that co-occur with gesture.

Captive apes

The primate family includes a large and diverse number of living species. This family arose over 50 million years ago, and includes modern lemurs, lorises, and gibbons as well as apes more closely related to humans including chimpanzees, bonobos, and gorillas (Tomasello and Call 1997). Primates are, on the whole, large-brained for body size, and sociable. As a general rule, as you get closer to humans in this family you get larger brains and more elaborate sensorimotor systems.

From the middle of the twentieth century there was a proliferation of attempts to train individual primates to communicate with humans. These programmes of study needed to sidestep the fact that non-human primates are not physiologically capable of producing speech. The human vocal tract is distinct for both its length and its articulators that require fine motor control. To circumvent the fact that other apes cannot vocalize like humans, many of these projects used manual communicative strategies, often a modified form of ASL or other signed language. Not all apes in this era of research were trained to use manual signed communication, Kanzi the bonobo used a board full of small unique symbols ('lexigrams') to communicate. By about six months of age he could use around 150 of them in response to speech or human use of the lexigrams.

Koko (1971–2018) the gorilla, and chimpanzees Washoe (1965–2007) and Nim Chimpsky (1973–2000), are three primates who were given linguistic input and studied for their communicative ability in the manual modality. There are some commonalities across the experience of all these trained primates, and the research programmes they found themselves participating in. The first is that their socialization was very different to, say, a child being raised in a signing household. The sign systems they learnt were something approaching a signed language, but none exhibited even a toddler's capacity for linguistic structure. While some communicative feats do seem impressive, these were not always able to be validated or replicated by people beyond a select research team. This research model was stopped because of its stressful impact on these primates, and while the research was not gestural in aim, it did indicate that apes can use manual action intentionally and communicatively.

More modern work with primates has not attempted to raise them to emulate human language acquisition, but instead focused more on attempting to map the nature of the specific capacity of non-human primate communication. For example Tomasello (2006) notes that in the extensive observational record, chimpanzees and other apes do not use deictic gestures with each other, although they can be trained to use these gestures with humans. Tomasello argues this is because humans are unique in their capacity for modelling the knowledge state of others. It is a good reminder that we should not assume that common functions or categories of human gesture will also be found in the communication of other species. Hobaiter and Byrne (2014) discuss four examples of what they argue is whole hand pointing by wild juvenile chimpanzees. This highlights the value of studying chimpanzees and other apes in their own social context, and that when it comes to ape gestures the picture is increasingly complex and nuanced. Rather than focusing on how individual primates communicate with humans, more recent research has been observing how they communicate with each other in their own natural social setting.

Wild apes

A series of studies of sustained observation have been conducted with groups of gorillas, chimpanzee, orangutans, and bonobo that live in social groups in their natural habitat (often in captive facilities) and have minimal interaction with humans (Byrne et al. 2017). All of these apes use gesture, and they use it deliberately with an intended audience. Overall, ape gestures are more intentional, communicative, and complex than their vocalizations. This communication is called gestural because it lacks any of the structural features of a language. There is a relatively large repertoire of gestures that have been documented, although the intended meanings are 'relatively few and simple' (in the words of Byrne et al. 2017: 755). The repertoires of different groups in different species have been compared and show extensive similarities, even across species. The shared repertoire shows multiple possible gestures for the same function, which adds to the flexibility of this communicative system. For example, in a systematic analysis of chimpanzee gestures, Hobaiter and Byrne (2011a) observed 4,397 intentional gestures over 266 days, which they were able to group into 66 distinct gesture types, many also used by captive chimps, as well as gorillas and orangutans.

While there is variation between different populations, there are many commonalities, and variation is not idiosyncratic. This strongly suggests a genetic inheritance of this communicative repertoire rather than it being the product of spontaneous creation in each group. Unlike human language, where vocabulary is expanded across a lifetime, younger apes will explore a wide possible range of gestures and narrow down to the active repertoire of the group as they mature. That the human-socialized apes discussed earlier managed to learn novel communicative gestures indicates that this system is flexible and not exclusively inherited. All of this evidence suggests that apes are born with a communicative capacity. The work of Byrne et al. (2017) has challenged an earlier hypothesis that ape gestures were the result of each generation turning functional behaviour into intentional signals, a theory known as 'ontogenetic ritualization'.

Although these gestural systems do not show any structuring that we would recognize as analogous to human language, recordings and observations have been made of multi-gesture sequences. Rather than being a sign of communicative sophistication, Hobaiter and Byrne (2011b) have shown that for chimpanzees these sequences tend to be used by younger chimps, who have not yet learnt which gesture(s) would be most efficient in a particular interaction. Indeed, juveniles use more gestures overall, not just in sequences. These strings of gestures tend to be less successful at evoking the desired reaction than single gestures. Hobaiter and Byrne (2011b) refer to this as 'repertoire tuning'.

Other animals

So far we have focused on great apes, but primates are not the only animals to consider when we look at evidence of gesture comprehension. We could take a very expansive view of what counts as gesture comprehension in the wider animal kingdom. If we think about deictic gestures and spatially pointing to a reference, the bee waggle dance tells its hivemates the direction where honey may be found. If we consider the different limb configuration of non-primates and look at the ability to track gaze instead of manual motions, then we find the capacity to track human gaze in a wide range of animals, including corvids such as crows and ravens. The complex set of skills that underpin our capacity for gesture are found, in part, across the animal kingdom (Fitch et al. 2010).

A growing body of research has illustrated that a number of animals have some capacity for comprehending human gesture (Shepherd 2010 provides a good summary). Domesticated dogs have been shown to have greater faculty for comprehending human gestures than their wild wolf cousins. Dogs can also successfully direct human attention. Dogs (*Canis familiaris*) were domesticated around ten to fifteen thousand years ago. Domestication and sustained contact with humans appears to have resulted in dogs' capacity to use pointing, gaze, and novel arbitrary communicative gestures to such an extent that MacLean et al. (2014) suggest their skills are approaching those of human children. Cats can also follow human pointing gestures made with an extended index finger, but they are less successful at directing human attention to a specific target (Miklósi et al. 2005). Shepherd also outlines evidence for pointing gesture comprehension by other domesticated mammals including goats and horses.

The capacity for following human pointing gestures has also been observed in dolphins and seals (Miklósi and Soproni 2006). Unlike domesticated animals, cetaceans have not had millennia to learn to communicate with humans and, unlike primates, they do not have arms they can use in their own-species communication that could also be used to communicate with humans. Comprehension of human gesture by marine mammals as well as domesticated animals suggests there may be more general communicative skills that underpin some of the gesturing documented for great apes and humans.

Gesture as part of language evolution

Now that we have seen how human gesture shares some features with the communicative skills of other species, we can return to focus specifically on how the human system, including gesture, arose. We will focus on the debate around the 'gesture-first' theories of language evolution, as this is where gesture has, unsurprisingly, contributed most to the discussion. Gesture-first theories of language do overlap with other theories. For example, these theories can sit alongside the language-from-grunts or language-from-singing theories on the premise that gesture started as the communicative load bearer before being surpassed by accompanying vocalizations. Gesture-first can be considered as a continuity theory of language evolution; gesture is one of the key skills that came together to build into what we now think of as the system of human language.

The basic premise of the gesture-first theory is that human language was scaffolded from gestures that were an earlier pre-linguistic form of communication (Corballis 2013). This theory challenged common earlier theories that language arose from calling behaviour. As a theory it respects the complex role that the manual modality plays in a variety of human and non-human contexts. We will look at evidence that is used to support this theory, including great ape gesture, language acquisition, and neurological evidence, all of which have been introduced in earlier sections of this book and in addition, the prevalence of hand stencils and prints in rock art from a range of the world's earliest documented civilizations. In particular, the hand stencils in the Cosquer Cave in France have been noted for the frequency of missing fingers, which have been interpreted by some as gestural representation, alongside images of humans and animals (Bouissac 2013).

The first piece of evidence looks at the communicative skill set of our closest living relatives. As we saw above in this chapter, chimpanzees, gorillas, and other great apes have a shared repertoire of gestures that are used intentionally and flexibly to achieve communicative goals. That some apes have been taught limited manual signing by humans suggests it is an adaptable system. Great apes appear to share a repertoire of gestures, which are then refined to a subset of active use within a specific social group (Byrne et al. 2017). A study of the gestures of one- and two-year-old children suggests that many of the gestures in this repertoire are also exhibited as human behaviour, at least in the early stages of language development (Kersken et al. 2019). Looking at thirteen children from two different cultural contexts (Uganda and Germany) the researchers found that 89 per cent of the fifty-two observed gestures by children were found in the documented ape repertoire. It is important that we do not assume that human language development in the individual goes through the same stages as the history of human language evolution at a population level (sometimes known in discussions of evolution as the 'recapitulation fallacy'), but the work of Kersken et al. (2019) highlights a commonality between ape gesturing and the gestures of human children before our linguistic systems are fully developed. We may also see evidence that the system of communicative gestures used by great apes is still accessible to adult humans; over five thousand adult humans did better than chance at guessing the function of the ten most common gestures used by chimpanzees and bonobos (Graham and Hobaiter 2023).

This study of infant gesture brings us to our second genre of evidence for the gesture-first hypothesis; language development in a variety of different human populations. At a similar time that scholarly societies were trying to dampen enthusiasm for discussions about the origins of language, the Second International Congress on Education of the Deaf in 1880 (commonly known as the Milan Congress) passed a resolution banning the use of signed language as a method of deaf education. It has been more than a century of work to reverse the damaging impact of this resolution, and the harmful effects of 'oralism' are still present in much deaf education today. Since the Milan Congress, we have overwhelming evidence that signed languages are, indeed, languages, and rich exposure to language of any modality is vital for children's development. In Chapter 5 we also saw how deaf individuals and their households can create homesign systems, and larger village sign systems can also arise. The documentation of the development of languages such as Nicaraguan Sign Language further demonstrates the capacity for signed systems, with an untold number of such languages undocumented across human history. Of course, the children in Nicaragua and people in all other recent contexts where signed languages or homesign systems have arisen, have benefited from having the human capacity for language in place, which is very different to an evolutionary development step. We do not want to conflate gesture and sign simply because of a shared modality. That said, that human language can be fully expressed in the manual modality has led some to argue that it may even have been the dominant mode of language at some point in history; gesture moving to something with more structural complexity as hominid brains became more complex.

The final broad area of evidence that has been used to argue for a gesture-first theory of language evolution comes from the human brain. In Chapter 6 we saw how the neurological capacity for gesture and language are largely co-located in the brain. It has been argued that the language centres grew out of earlier capacity for gesture. Mirror neurons, that activate both when performing an action and when watching someone else perform an action, have been posited as an mechanism for how gestural capacity was developed, and then co-opted into a more generalized (and eventual non-manual) language capacity. A gestural origin of language could also explain how, for example, there is such a strong neural link between the movement of the mouth and the hands (Vainio 2019).

There is evidence from human brains, human language acquisition, and non-human communicative systems, that gesture is a central part of the story of human language evolution. A key question, one that can only really remain speculative, is why was there a shift of modality from manual to verbal? Suggestions have included that human hands became too busy with tools, or humans wanted to communicate in the absence of light or direct line of sight, while some have argued that the move to verbal communication can form part of the explanation for the rise in human material culture, including everything from bodily ornamentation to art to tools (Corballis 2013). Although it is important not to treat modern human cultures that use signed languages as indicative of evolutionary history, it is worth noting that these cultures manage both to use manual signs and to participate in material culture practices (Emmorey 2005). As Emmorey notes, we also have no historical evidence of a signed language arising in any context except deaf communities.

Although it is clear that gesture is a key part of modern human language, and the communication of our near relatives, understanding its exact role in the development of human language is an ongoing challenge. Gesture-first models can generally be considered to be continuity models, but not everyone agrees this is the case. McNeill (2012) argues that we can use our understanding of how gesture is currently used in human communication to see the limits of an argument for the gestural origins of language. The gesture-first model suggests that a manual mode of interaction was replaced with a verbal mode, which would mean that gestures are now superfluous. The research from McNeill and many others discussed in this book shows how gesture is, in fact, a deeply integrated feature of human language, not additional to it. This would mean that a gesture-first model of language evolution is more of a discontinuity theory, and needs to account for how gesture continued to play the communicative role that it has.

The future of gesture

To understand the future of gesture, we must include more than humans and animals. We are now communicating through, and with, increasingly sophisticated machines. In Chapter 2 we saw just how important the creation of affordable video recording in the twentieth century was to the development of Gesture Studies. If you have a mobile phone, it is very likely that the video recording capability of your pocket-sized device would have been the envy of most researchers working in the field in the 1980s. We now make video calls, consume studio-quality video content made by people in their homes, and find ourselves in ever-more-immersive video games, sometimes in virtual reality.

Anything we have to say about the specifics of gesture and technology will be outdated by the next generation of hardware and user interfaces. What we can do is plot a general history of technology and gesture. We will start by thinking about how technology has changed the way we gesture to each other, then consider how we gesture to our screens and devices, before thinking about how the machines are gesturing back. The future is here, and the future is multimodal.

Gesturing to each other online

The 1968 film *2001: A Space Odyssey* gave us a vision of a high-tech future in the prosaic moment Dr Heywood Floyd calls home using a public phonebooth on a space station. It is made clear to us that it is the future because of the minimalist décor and the fact he is on a lunar space station, but also because this is a video call. His young daughter is able to see him shake his head when he tells her he won't be home for her birthday party, and he can see that her mother is currently out, and the babysitter is busy (the implication being that the video technology is so easy a child can use it). Kubrick's vision was slightly premature, video calling really took off a decade or so later than the turn of the century, but the vision was also somewhat insufficient; the rise of the mobile telephone means that we do not have to find a public booth to make a video call.

Telephones have been with us for around 150 years, but we are only just entering the era of video interaction. What effect this will have on our gesturing practice as the technology continues to improve is very much an open question. We have seen in earlier chapters that speakers will shape their gestures to their audience, and so it is likely there are features of video interaction that will shape the way we gesture. Gullberg and Holmsqvist (2006) used eye-tracking in one study and found that the audience fixated on speaker gestures less in video than face-to-face, even when the video was on a life-size screen, and even if the speaker looked at their own gesture. Video calls may be more multimodal than audio-only, but it appears that gaze requirements are not quite the same as in face-to-face interaction.

While we have settled into the new normal of online video interaction, people have been experimenting with ways to bring us together in an embodied online space. Virtual reality (VR) aims to simulate the immersive experience of physical space in a digital environment. The most basic VR systems involve wearing goggles that simulate a three dimensional environment; even the earliest and most basic systems can provoke a fear response when walking across a pixelated plank between skyscrapers. While graphics have rapidly improved, the way we interact with these systems has been slower to evolve. Some of the most sophisticated systems will map user gestures with some precision, but many consumer-grade systems still limit input to a basic 'trigger' for each hand and limited head and body movement. As of the mid-2020s, virtual reality systems have found a niche for video gamers, but have yet to become common for any other form of entertainment. Current state-of-the-art

VR systems with body, face, and finger tracking show that, compared to video-conferencing, people use more deictic gestures, and less non-gestural self-touching (usually treated as a proxy for self-consciousness), suggesting people feel more like they are in the same space (Abdullah et al. 2021). How these systems manage gesture and other features of natural human interaction will likely influence their future in social or professional domains. For now, the cheap ubiquity of video, and the easy multimodal affordances it allows, appears to have won out.

The rise of video and audio on the internet do not diminish the large volumes of written content that are still consumed online. While we measure the development of speech-at-a-distance in decades, we can measure the development of language-at-a-distance in millennia with writing created at least three different times 2000–5000 years ago (in Mesopotamia, China, and Meso-America). Writing is so dominant in our understanding of language that in literate societies it has skewed the focus towards the structures that are captured by these systems. The rise of the internet has also seen a profusion of new, informal, and playful ways of using writing, with a new multimodality arising (McCulloch 2019). These new conventions are an element of a general capacity for using graphic symbols and structures as part of our multimodal communicative repertoire (Cohn and Schilperoord 2024). One digital communication strategy is the use of emoticons and emojis. Emoticons repurpose existing characters and punctuation, often to create facial expressions to indicate the tone of a written message. The now classic smiley uses a colon and a right bracket (with an optional dash for a nose) to indicate a sideways smiling face, and a positive sentiment :). Emoticons that scan horizontally rather than vertically (e.g.: ^–^) are known by the Japanese term 'kaomoji' (lit. 'face characters'). As can be seen from our examples, the Japanese kaomoji tend to have more elaborate eyes, and the Western emoticons have more elaborate mouths, which parallels the difference in focus in drawing facial expressions in Japanese Manga and Western Comics (Cohn and Ehly 2016).

Alongside emoticons has come the rise of emojis in online communication. Unlike emoticons and kaomojis, emojis are distinct character elements, rather than repurposed characters. Emoji are small images that are encoded for digital use in the same way as the punctuation and characters in the world's writing system. This means that they are images, but they are as easy to send as any typed letter of the alphabet; both in terms of the data required and in terms of keyboard typing. What is included in the emoji set is decided by Unicode, a consortium of technology companies that agrees on the standard text format for all of the world's written scripts, symbols, and also emojis. This means that the same set of emojis can be shared across devices, something that was not always guaranteed for any text before Unicode started its work in the late 1980s. Unicode version 16.0 from 2024 includes 3,790 emojis. The Unicode emoji set includes a wide range of animals, plants, buildings, symbols, emotive faces, and humans doing activities. There are also a range of hands in various gestures. I have been a member of Unicode's Emoji Standard and Research Working Group, helping to improve the processes by which new emojis are proposed, and thinking about a more cross-culturally diverse approach to gestures in emoji form. This included, for example, making sure that the head nodding and shaking gestures introduced in Unicode 15.1 in 2023, had neutral facial expressions in recognition that nodding is only an affirmative gesture in Western cultures, and in other parts of the world can be a neutral or negative action.

The gesture emojis are mostly identifiable as a range of pointing and emblems. This is perhaps unsurprising when we consider that both of these categories of gesture have identifiable meanings based on specific forms. This reliable recognizability means that gestures are one of the most often used category of emojis. When we look at the most frequently used emojis we see faces, hearts, and hands make up the list. Table 4 is the list of most frequently used emojis in 2022 (Unicode 2023).

Two manual emblems are in the top ten emojis. The first is the 'thumbs up'. This emoji has long been used to indicate an affirmative across Western countries (Morris et al. 1979). Thanks to the use of the thumbs up on social media (particularly Facebook) as a mechanism to 'like' content, the thumbs up is now ubiquitous. In some countries more in the Arabic and/or Islamic sphere, including Jordan and Bangladesh, the thumbs up is traditionally a taboo emblem of offence, analogous to the middle finger

Table 4 The ten most commonly used emojis in 2022 according to Unicode

Frequency rank	Emoji	Name
1	😂	Face with tears of joy
2	❤️	Red heart
3	🤣	Rolling on the floor laughing
4	👍	Thumbs up
5	😭	Loudly crying face
6	🙏	Folded hands
7	😘	Face blowing a kiss
8	🥰	Smiling face with hearts
9	😍	Smiling face with heart eyes
10	😊	Smiling face with smiling eyes

in Western contexts. The ubiquity of the social media thumbs up means that these two emblems now coexist, and the online emblem is more common with younger people. The second emblem is the emoji known as 'folded hands' most commonly used to mean 'thank you'. While this has been one use of this emblem in Western contexts, it has been more traditionally used to indicate Christian prayer or begging. The interactional need for a clear and legible way to indicate thanks in emoji form has resulted in the rise of this emoji.

Not only are there some emojis that visually replicate common gestures, many of the ways that we use emojis alongside writing parallel the way that we use gestures with our speech. We can add visual content that is integrated into the stream of text in ways that are much easier than in pre-digital writing. In work with my colleague Gretchen McCulloch (Gawne and McCulloch 2019), we mapped the use of emojis onto the properties of gesture outlined in Chapter 2, and looked at how emojis perform similar functions to the different categories of gesture we met in Chapter 3. The rise of informal writing has allowed some features of multimodality to resurface in text. We also see this with the trend for using custom 'sticker' images and GIFs (compressed sets of images that play as short looping videos), often used as a reaction in a text-based interaction. Different social media platforms have also introduced their own images that act like emojis on their specific apps. While they only work in that particular ecosystem, they are not limited to the official Unicode set, allowing for personalization for each group. Whether these represent a next-phase for communication online, or are just another playful fad, people will continue to play with multimodality in writing as well as speech.

Gesturing with machines

The earliest computers were decidedly disembodied; we communicated with them through switches, punch cards, and written language commands. From the 1980s onwards, graphical user interfaces allowed for the use of spatial inputs, like the mouse, and improvements in touchscreens have further reduced the physical distance between the movement input and resultant action. Beyond the hands as input, phones can now use smile detection and hand gestures to take photographs, and augmented and virtual reality systems can track a user's movements in physical space. Improvements in the fidelity of these input systems will further reduce the gap between interacting with physical and digital spaces and the way we interact with smart devices in our homes, and offices, and cars (Wu et al. 2023). When it comes to gesturing to machines, special mention needs to go to the Kinect. This was a peripheral made by Microsoft as a motion-tracking input, mostly for the Xbox 360 and Xbox One between 2010 and 2017. The technology is now integrated into other Microsoft products, but it has a special place as a research tool in Gesture Studies for being relatively accurate for its affordability (e.g., Trujillo et al. 2019).

Improvements in our ability to interact with computers have been paralleled by improvements in their output. Computers process video and animated graphics of constantly-improving quality, and motion capture of live performances has an added dimension of naturalness to 3D animation. Even without these developments, it takes relatively little rendering detail for the gestures of humanoid digital avatars to be useful for their human conversation partners. NUMACK, a digital, blue polygon-bodied humanoid robot, was better at conveying directional information when using listener-oriented gestures, than when using no gestures, or gestures oriented towards itself (Hasegawa et al. 2010). The challenge of creating realistic embodied conversational agents (ECA) is taking something that humans do with great variation, as we have seen throughout this book, and turning it into something that is programmable for non-humans (Cassell 2007). A variety of coding options have been created, and machine learning applications are being developed. ECAs may not replace the voice- or text-based chat systems that we have become used to any time soon, but they are enriching video games, and are being developed for custom educational, commercial, and therapeutic uses.

Some of the work on the way our technology gestures to us has been done in the physical space with dexterous and interactive robots. In 2014 Honda's ASIMO (first launched in the year 2000 after decades of development) had jointed fingers with enough degrees of freedom to use the ASL fingerspelling alphabet, albeit very very slowly. De Wit (2022) found that while gesturing was a key way to make interacting with robots successful, often the robot programmers and engineers did not always have good models for how to do this, indeed over 40 per cent of the papers in de Wit's review of the topic did not draw on any observations from the Gesture Studies literature. Research indicates that robots that gesture are perceived to be more likeable or enthusiastic, and de Wit's own work designing robots to help Dutch-speaking four-to six-year-olds learn English has shown that engagement increased when the robot used iconic gestures, although a positive effect on word memorization was not always shown. At this stage of technological advancement, it is very unlikely that we will be dealing with a robot uprising using rich multimodal negotiations; the SoftBank NAO robot used by de Wit still needs to be coded by a human to gesture, and the ASIMO project was suspended in early 2022.

Whether we are interacting with each other, physical robots, or digital avatars, our interactions are increasingly mediated by technologies. Some of these technologies will account for gesture better than others, and will open up new avenues for understanding how we interact multimodally.

Conclusion

Debates regarding the origin of language have historically been held with highly speculative evidence. There are many theories proposed for the origins of human language, and one of those theories is that communication started as gestures first. Early work with great apes attempted to teach formal linguistic systems, including modified signed languages, to limited success. In their own social contexts, great apes have flexible and intentionalized systems of communicative gestures. These show commonalities across chimpanzees, orangutans, bonobos, and gorillas, suggesting an inherited system. Domesticated animals and wild cetaceans have shown a capacity to interact with human gestures, suggesting some of the underlying cognitive skills are not just found in primates closely related to humans. In the debates about the origins of human language, proponents of the gesture-first theories have drawn on evidence from great ape gestures, child language development, homesign and village sign systems, and the close neurological relationship between hand and mouth as evidence of the gestural underpinnings of language. Gesture and sign language specialists have been keen to point out that these theories still do not clarify why the verbal modality came to dominate human language, nor explain how gesture is still highly integrated into this system.

Looking to the future of how we gesture, the rise of ubiquitous video interaction provides a new domain for gesture, one where the audience gaze is less predictable in terms of attention to gesture. Digital interaction has also opened up multimodal written communication, including emojis, GIFs, and stickers, which show parallels to the use of gesture with speech. Embodied conversational agents in the digital domain, and robots in the physical domain, are also gesturing back to us, although these are still highly programmed interactions.

Further reading and resources

The Many Minds podcast helps place human cognition in the wider context of the diversity of minds in this world. Two episodes are particularly relevant to this chapter. The first is an interview with Michael Tomasello (Of chimps and children[1]), and the second is an interview with Cat Hobaiter (How do chimps communicate?[2]). We touched on the work of both researchers in this chapter.

[1] https://manyminds.libsyn.com/of-chimps-and-children
[2] https://manyminds.libsyn.com/how-do-chimps-communicate

8

Conclusion

In the last half century, researchers in Gesture Studies have explored a wide range of questions from different disciplinary perspectives. The study of gesture is still a young field, and there is even more to explore in the coming decades. Gesture is not a monolithic phenomenon. It has a complex and contextual relationship to spoken and signed languages, a shifting role across the lifespan and a role in human language development that is still very much open for debate. Seemingly contradictory outcomes of existing research may, with more information, resolve themselves as we develop a more nuanced picture. Different gestures might have different functions in relation to the linguistic channel, and different functions in interaction. Different gestures might have different cognitive and neurological mechanisms. Different gestures may show different kinds of variation, in individuals, across populations, and across signed and spoken language modalities. When we add to this the fact that researchers in Gesture Studies come to the discipline from their own backgrounds, interests and methods, we begin to see a field that is still exploring the territory.

Some of our biggest open questions are due to the fact that the majority of work is still done with a very small number of languages and cultures (see Blasi et al. 2022 for a discussion of this issue in cognitive science more generally). I have tried to highlight the range of different cultural and linguistic contexts where work on gesture has been undertaken, but overall, you may have noticed particular languages and contexts recurring throughout this book, something which reflects the interests and expertise of the existing practitioners in the field.

Gesture. Lauren Gawne, Oxford University Press. © Lauren Gawne (2025).
DOI: 10.1093/9780198951377.003.0008

There are many advantages to the fact that Gesture Studies is a field with practitioners from a wide range of disciplines and countries. One of the advantages is that I have found scholars in this field to be incredibly welcoming of newcomers who have acquainted themselves with the basics, and are always excited to have people working on new questions, applying new methods, and broadening the field to new populations.

It is my hope that more people will contribute to building this richer picture of what gesture is and how it can be studied. There are so many ways you can contribute to the study of gesture without having to consider yourself a Gesture Studies scholar: linguists in language documentation and child language acquisition can include gesture in their descriptive work, computer systems researchers can think about truly multimodal systems, cognitive scientists can include gesture in their models of language, historians can help us to find the subtle traces of gesture in the written record.

In this Slim Guide introduction to the field of Gesture Studies, I hope I have provided a lightning tour of the fundamentals of how we describe gesture and key areas of research. Gesture is a part of human language, and has a stable and complex relationship with the linguistic structures of spoken and signed languages. Gesture shares a modality with other communicative systems, including emblems, pantomime, and signed languages, but they are very different in terms of structure and their integration with linguistic systems. Gesture Studies scholars have a generally-agreed upon set of gesture categories that draw on both formal and functional features of gesture, including iconic, metaphoric, deictic, recurrent, and beat gestures. Speakers use gesture to communicate and to structure thought, changing their use of gesture in response to the presence of an audience, and audiences use the information from gestures in processing speech. Gesture is part of some of our earliest communication, and shifts as we acquire new languages. Gesture is integrated with both motor and linguistic systems in the brain and needs to be accounted for in cognitive models of language production and processing. Gesture appears to have been part of hominid communication that predates language, but the relationship between gesture and the origin of linguistic structure is complicated.

I still remember one conversation with Barb Kelly, many years after that first introduction to Gesture Studies, after I had completed my PhD project and had started to look at the use of gesture in my recordings from Nepal (what would eventually be Gawne 2018 and 2021). I was complaining of my frustration with an element of the analysis I was stuck on. She told me about a moment during her own PhD research when she realized that her analysis of children interacting with their caregivers had not given any serious attention to what was happening with the gestures. She was already some months into coding and attempting to analyse the data, and the realization that she would have to rethink her approach made her want to cry. Understanding the contribution of gesture in early language acquisition was the key to making sense of what she was seeing in her data. She would go on to make important observations about the speech + gesture combinations she was seeing in her data and provide us with a richer understanding of the transition children make between the one word and two-word phases of language acquisition. I shared this work in Chapter 5. I have often thought about Barb's experience while writing this book. It is my hope that this introduction to the field of Gesture Studies will help scholars, at all stages of their careers, consider the contribution of gesture to the work that they are doing, and hopefully early enough to build in a multimodal perspective from the outset. I hope that you will now see the richness of multimodal human communication.

Further reading and resources

I hope that the references throughout this book have provided you with many starting points to your own exploration and research. The best way to keep up to date with research in the field of Gesture Studies is to join the International Society for Gesture Studies. The ISGS has a mailing list, hosts conferences every two years, and provides a community for an international network of scholars from across disciplines. The ISGS is also responsible for the publication of the journal *Gesture*, which publishes three issues a year.

Glossary

Alternative sign language A signed language that is used alongside a spoken language in a community with both deaf and hearing members. See Chapter 2.

Analytic Units of language can be broken into smaller meaningful units. This is one of the features of linguistic systems that is not a feature of gesture. Gesture does not have consistent, meaningful substructures but is more synthetic. Cf. Synthetic. See Chapter 2.

Apex The phase of a gesture stroke when the hand or head or other part of the body is the most extended or articulated. Also known as the peak. See Chapter 2.

Aphasia Language production or processing impairment due to damage to the relevant region(s) of the brain. See Chapter 6.

ASL American Sign Language.

Auslan Australian Sign Language.

Auxiliary sign system A limited system of manual signs that emerges in contexts where (usually hearing) people are unable to verbally communicate, e.g. scuba hand signs, umpire signals. See Chapter 2.

Baton Another term for beat gestures.

Beat A gesture with a repetitious action used for emphasis. See Chapter 3.

Biphasic The distinctive stroke pattern of a beat gesture that involves a repetition of movement at the apex of the stroke for the duration of the gesture performance. See Chapter 3.

Broca's aphasia Damage to Broca's area that results in difficulties in the production of speech and gesture, even though comprehension is maintained. See Chapter 6.

Broca's area A region (usually) in the left frontal lobe of the human brain that plays a role in the production of complex linguistic structures. See Chapter 6.

BSL British Sign Language.

Co-speech gestures the gestures that we make alongside speech, the relationship to speech and context is what makes their meaning comprehensible. See Chapters 2 and 3.

Combinatoric Language can combine meaningful elements to create more complex meaning. This is one of the features of linguistic systems that is not a feature of gesture, which is described as 'non-combinatoric'. Cf. non-combinatoric. See Chapter 2.

Context-independent Language has stable meaning independent of the specific context of use. This is one of the features of linguistic systems that is not a feature of gesture, which is context-sensitive. Cf. Context sensitive. See Chapter 2.

Context-sensitive Gesture is context-sensitive in contrast with linguistic systems, because language has a stable meaning independent of context. Cf. Context-independent. See Chapter 2.

Continuity theory Theories of the origins of human language which propose that language is so complex, the only explanation for its origin is that it arose from existing earlier pre-linguistic systems. See Chapter 7.

Deictic A gesture that indicates the location of a place or object. See Chapter 3.

Depiction An iconic gesture that depicts some physical property of an object by sketching our outlining the size or shape or another property. See Chapter 3.

Depictive gesture Another term for iconic gestures.

Discontinuity theory Theories of the origins of human language that propose that language is so complex, and so unique in the animal kingdom, that the only explanation for its origin is that it arose suddenly and all at once. See Chapter 7.

Emblem A gesture that has a fixed form–meaning relationship for a specific community of users. Examples include the thumbs up, OK gesture, and head nod. See Chapter 3.

Embodied Conversational Agent A humanoid digital avatar that aims to provide a naturalistic interactional partner for multimodal communication. See Chapter 7.

Embodiment An approach to understanding human behaviour that sees human thought, language, and experience as fundamentality tied to the physical reality of existing as embodied beings.

Enactment An iconic gesture where the gesturer takes the role of the target person or object. See Chapter 3.

Gesticulation Another term for co-speech gesture.

Gesture the intentional communicative movement of the body, most notably the hands, usually in the context of spoken or signed language. Sometimes used to refer specifically to co-speech gestures.

Gesture as simulated action A cognitive model of the relationship of speech and gesture production, where spatial and action features of language activate motor function and spill over into gesture. See Chapter 6.

Gesture continuum A way of representing the relationship between co-speech gestures and other communicative bodily actions, including pantomime, emblems, and signed languages. See Chapter 2.

Gesture for conceptualization A cognitive model of the relationship of speech and gesture production, where the schematic nature of gesture is used in the conceptualization of action and language. See Chapter 6.

Gesture phase A segment of the articulation of a given gesture, includes preparation, stroke, and holds. See Chapter 2.

Gesture phrase All of the phases that constitute a single gesture. Individual gesture phrases can build into larger gesture units. See Chapter 2.

Gesture space The physical space in which a person will extend their arms and hands to gesture, includes the centre, mid-range, and peripheral spaces. See Chapter 2.

Gesture unit The series of gesture phrases that are articulated between periods of rest. Multiple gesture phrases combine to form a gesture unit. See Chapter 2.

Global Gestures do not have complex structures that have hierarchies, but their meaning is taken from the whole gesture. This is in contrast with linguistic systems, because language is hierarchical. Cf. Hierarchical. See Chapter 2.

Growth point A cognitive model of the relationship of speech and gesture production, where gesture and speech are conceptualized together in a pre-linguistic stage of thought known as the 'growth point'. See Chapter 6.

Handshape The configuration of fingers and hand in the performance of a sign in a signed language or a gesture.

Hierarchical Language has hierarchical structures that allow for embedding and complex grammar. This is one of the features of linguistic systems that is not a feature of gesture, which is global in its structure. Cf. Global. See Chapter 2.

Hold Maintenance of a gesture apex for any duration of time. An optional phase of gesture performance that can occur before or after the stroke of the gesture. See Chapter 2.

Homesign A highly restricted sign system that can emerge in households where a deaf child is raised in a hearing family without exposure to signed language input. See Chapter 5.

Horizontal plane One of the different directions away from the torso that a person can move to perform a gesture. This is the plane across the body from a person's left to their right. Also known as the lateral plane. See Chapter 2.

Iconic gesture A gesture that depicts the physical properties of things in the world. See Chapter 3.

Interface model A cognitive model of the relationship of speech and gesture production, where a language formulator influences the gesture formulator to shape the structure of gesture. See Chapter 6.

Kinesics The study of the movement of the human body, of which gesture is one component. See Chapter 2.

Kinetographic gesture Another term for iconic gestures.

L1 First language(s). The first language(s) a child is exposed to in their development. See Chapter 5.

L2 Second language(s). Languages that are learnt after the early years exposure to a child's first language(s). See Chapter 5.

Lateral plane Another term for the horizontal plane.

Lexical retrieval hypothesis The theory that gesturing helps activate the mental lexicon in a way that assists word retrieval during periods of disfluency. See Chapter 5.

Manner-verb language A language where lexical verbs tend to include information about the manner of a movement, with information about the path of the movement included with additional lexical items. See Chapter 4.

Manual In Gesture Studies, typically used to refer to gestures made with the hands, in contrast with gestures made with the head, shoulders, legs, or other articulators.

Metaphoric gesture A gesture that depicts an abstract concept as having physical properties. For example, a gesture that represents the abstract concept of time spatially so that the past is on the left of the speaker. See Chapter 3.

Mirror neurons Neurons that activate when a person performs an action, or watches someone perform that action. See Chapter 6.

Modelling An iconic gesture that models some element of the object being depicted. See Chapter 3.

Motor cortex The part of the brain responsible for the movement of the body. See Chapter 6.

Multimodal Pertaining to more than one 'mode' of production. Can be used to distinguish speech and gesture, or in sign to distinguish between linguistic content and gestural content. Is also sometimes used, e.g. in 'multimodal multilingual', to distinguish people who are proficient in both a signed and spoken language.

Non-combinatoric This is in contrast with linguistic systems, because language is combinatoric while gestures are not. Cf. Combinatoric. See Chapter 2.

Oralism An ideology where there is a preference for not introducing a deaf child to an existing signed language. See Chapter 5.

Pantomime Imitations of actions that can briefly come to have a stable meaning in a limited context. See Chapter 2.

Path-verb language A language where lexical verbs tend to include information about the path of a movement, with information about the manner of the movement included with additional lexical items. See Chapter 4.

Peak Another term for the apex of a gesture.

Phonological alignment The apex of a gestural stroke tends to occur with, or slightly before, the phonologically prominent syllable of a spoken language. See Chapter 2.

Pictographic Another term for iconic gestures.

Pointing Another term for deictic gestures.

Post-stroke hold A pause in movement between the preparation and the stroke of a gesture. See Chapter 2.

Pragmatic gesture A gesture that has a meaning that relates to the pragmatic or discourse level of the interaction. Also known as recurrent gestures. See Chapter 3.

Pre-stroke hold A pause in movement between the stroke of a gesture and the recovery or preparation for the next gesture. See Chapter 2.

Preparation The movement leading up to the stroke of the gesture. See Chapter 2.

Pronation The movement of rotation of the forearm, which causes the palm of the hand to be facing down (prone). See Chapter 2.

Prone Facing downward. For example, the hand is prone when the palm is facing downward. See Chapter 2.

Recovery After the stroke of the gesture, the hand returns to rest. This is optional, as the person may commence another gesture. Also known as retraction. See Chapter 2.

Recurrent gesture Another term for pragmatic gestures.

Rest The body is not in any phase of performing a gesture. See Chapter 2.

Retraction Another term for the recovery phase.

Sagittal plane One of the different directions away from the torso that a person can move to perform a gesture. Moves out in front of the speaker from the centre, and behind. See Chapter 2.

Semantic alignment Gesture and co-occurring speech align in their meaning. See Chapter 2.

Sensorimotor The cognitive integration of movement and perception. Often 'sensori-motor', sometimes 'sensory-motor'. See Chapter 6.

Sign language A language that uses hands and other parts of the body as articulators rather than the voice. Also signed language. See Chapter 2.

Sketch model A cognitive model of the relationship of speech and gesture production, where a conceptualizer includes a preverbal message for speech and a spatio-temporal sketch for gesture. See Chapter 6.

Source For metaphoric gestures, the domain from which the metaphor is borrowed to be applied to a target. See Chapter 3.

Spatio-temporal metaphor The use of physical space as a metaphor for the abstract concept of time. Gestures about time are often mapped onto spatial metaphors. Sometimes 'spatiotemporal'. See Chapter 4.

Stroke The most extended or prominent component of the gesture, the obligatory feature of a gesture around which all the other phases occur. It is typically where the meaning of a gesture is expressed and which aligns with any concurrent linguistic content. See Chapter 2.

Supine Facing upward. For example, the hand is supine when the palm is facing upward. See Chapter 2.

Synthetic This is in contrast with linguistic systems, because language is analytical. Cf. Analytic. See Chapter 2.

Target For metaphoric gestures, the domain that a metaphor is applied to from the source. See Chapter 3.

Vertical plane One of the different directions away from the torso that a person can move to perform a gesture. The vertical plane is from up above the head to down below the torso. See Chapter 2.

Viewpoint The perspective from which a gesture, particularly an iconic gesture, is performed. Viewpoints include observer viewpoint and participant viewpoint. See Chapter 3.

Village sign A signed system that emerges in a context where deaf people live in a social context with hearing people. Some village sign systems are full signed languages, often used by deaf and hearing community members alike. See Chapter 5.

Wernicke's aphasia Damage to Wernicke's area that results in difficulties in language comprehension. See Chapter 6.

Wernicke's area A region (usually) in the left temporal lobe of the human brain that plays a role in comprehension and content of speech. See Chapter 6.

References

Abdullah, Ahsan, Jan Kolkmeier, Vivian Lo, and Michael Neff. (2021). 'Videoconference and embodied VR: Communication patterns across task and medium', *Proceedings of the ACM on Human-Computer Interaction*, 5/CSCW2: 1–29. DOI: 10.1145/3479597

Allen, Shanley, Aslı Özyürek, Sotaro Kita, Amanda Brown, Reyhan Furman, Tomoko Ishizuka, and Mihoko Fujii. (2007). 'Language-specific and universal influences in children's syntactic packaging of Manner and Path: A comparison of English, Japanese, and Turkish', *Cognition*, 102/1: 16–48. DOI: 10.1016/j.cognition.2005.12.006

Andres, P., and M. Van der Linden. (2000). 'Age-related differences in supervisory attentional system functions', *The Journals of Gerontology Series B: Psychological Sciences and Social Sciences*, 55/6: P373–80. DOI: 10.1093/geronb/55.6.P373

Arbib, Michael A. (2013). 'Mirror systems and the neurocognitive substrates of bodily communication and language'. Cornelia Müller, Alan Cienki, Ellen Fricke, Silva Ladewig, David McNeill, and Sedinha Tessendorf (eds), *Body—Language—Communication: An International Handbook on Multimodality in Human Interaction*, Vol. 1, pp. 451–66. Berlin/Boston: De Gruyter. DOI: 10.1515/9783110261318.451

Astington, John H. (2006). 'Actors and the body: Meta-theatrical rhetoric in Shakespeare', *Gesture*, 6/2: 241–59.

Astuti, Rita. (1995). *People of the Sea: Identity and Descent among the Vezo of Madagascar*. Cambridge/New York: Cambridge University Press.

Aussems, Suzanne, and Sotaro Kita. (2019). 'Seeing iconic gestures while encoding events facilitates children's memory of these events', *Child Development*, 90/4: 1123–37. DOI: 10.1111/cdev.12988

Bagchi, Tista. (2010). 'The signing system of Mudra in traditional Indian dance', *Paragrana*, 19/1: 259–66. DOI: 10.1524/para.2010.0017

Barnes, R. H. (1973). 'The rainbow in the representations of inhabitants of the Flores area of Indonesia', *Anthropos*, 68/3/4: 611–13.

Bates, Elizabeth, Luigia Camaioni, and Virginia Volterra. (1975). 'The aquisition of performatives prior to speech', *Merrill-Palmer Quarterly of Behavior and Development*, 21/3: 205–26.

Bavelas, Janet Beavin, Nicole Chovil, Douglas A. Lawrie, and Allan Wade. (1992). 'Interactive gestures', *Discourse Processes*, 15/4: 469–89. DOI: 10.1080/01638539209544823

Bavelas, Janet, Jennifer Gerwing, Chantelle Sutton, and Danielle Prevost. (2008). 'Gesturing on the telephone: Independent effects of dialogue and visibility', *Journal of Memory and Language*, 58/2: 495–520. DOI: 10.1016/j.jml.2007.02.004

Beattie, Geoffrey. (2016). *Rethinking Body Language: How Hand Movements Reveal Hidden Thoughts*. New York: Routledge.

Beattie, Geoffrey, and Rima Aboudan. (1994). 'Gestures, pauses and speech: An experimental investigation of the effects of changing social context on their precise temporal relationships', *Semiotica*, 99/3–4: 239–72. DOI: 10.1515/semi.1994.99.3-4.239

Beaupoil-Hourdel, Pauline. (2021). 'Embodying language complexity: Co-speech gestures between age 3 and 4'. Aliyah Morgenstern and Susan Goldin-Meadow (eds), *Gesture in Language*, pp. 157–84. APA/De Gruyter: Washington DC/Berlin. DOI: 10.1515/9783110567526-007

ter Bekke, Marlijn, Linda Drijvers, and Judith Holler. (2020). 'The predictive potential of hand gestures during conversation: An investigation of the timing of gestures in relation to speech' (preprint). *PsyArXiv*. Retrieved 11 January 2024, from <osf.io/b5zq7>. DOI: 10.31234/osf.io/b5zq7

Birdwhistell, Ray L. (1970). *Kinesics and Context: Essays on Body Motion Communication*. Philadelphia: University of Pennsylvania Press.

Blasi, Damián E., Joseph Henrich, Evangelia Adamou, David Kemmerer, and Asifa Majid. (2022). 'Over-reliance on English hinders cognitive science', *Trends in Cognitive Sciences*, S1364661322002364. DOI: 10.1016/j.tics.2022.09.015

Blust, Robert. (2021). 'Pointing, rainbows, and the archaeology of mind', *Anthropos*, 116/1: 145–62. DOI: 10.5771/0257-9774-2021-1-145

Bosker, Hans Rutger, and David Peeters. (2021). 'Beat gestures influence which speech sounds you hear', *Proceedings of the Royal Society B: Biological Sciences*, 288/1943: 20202419. DOI: 10.1098/rspb.2020.2419

Bouissac, Paul. (2013). 'Prehistoric gestures: Evidence from artifacts and rock art'. Cornelia Müller, Alan Cienki, Ellen Fricke, Silva Ladewig, David McNeill, and Sedinha Tessendorf (eds), *Body—Language—Communication: An International Handbook on Multimodality in Human Interaction*, Vol. 1, pp. 301–6. Berlin/Boston: De Gruyter. DOI: 10.1515/9783110261318

Breckinridge Church, R., and Susan Goldin-Meadow. (1986). 'The mismatch between gesture and speech as an index of transitional knowledge', *Cognition*, 23/1: 43–71. DOI: 10.1016/0010-0277(86)90053-3

Bressem, Jana, and Cornelia Müller. (2014). 'A repertoire of German recurrent gestures with pragmatic functions'. Cornelia Müller, Silva Ladewig, Alan J. Cienki, Ellen Fricke, David McNeill, and Jana Bressem (eds), *Body—language—Communication: An International Handbook on Multimodality in Human Interaction*, pp. 1575–91. Berlin/Boston: De Gruyter Mouton.

Bressem, Jana, Nicole Stein, and Claudia Wegener. (2017). 'Multimodal language use in Savosavo: Refusing, excluding and negating with speech and gesture', *Pragmatics*, 27/2: 173–206. DOI: 10.1075/prag.27.2.01bre

Brône, Geert, Bert Oben, Annelies Jehoul, Jelena Vranjes, and Kurt Feyaerts. (2017). 'Eye gaze and viewpoint in multimodal interaction management', *Cognitive Linguistics*, 28/3: 449–83. DOI: 10.1515/cog-2016-0119

Brookes, Heather. (2004). 'A repertoire of South African quotable gestures', *Journal of Linguistic Anthropology*, 14/2: 186–224.

Brown, Amanda, and Marianne Gullberg. (2008). 'Bidirectional crosslinguistic influence in L1-L2 encoding of manner in speech and gesture: A study of Japanese speakers of English', *Studies in Second Language Acquisition*, 30/2: 225–51. DOI: 10.1017/S0272263108080327

Brown, Penelope, and Stephen C. Levinson. (1987). *Politeness: Some Universals in Language Usage*. Cambridge/New York: Cambridge University Press.

Butterworth, Brian, and Geoffrey Beattie. (1978). 'Gesture and silence as indicators of planning in speech'. Robin N. Campbell, and Philip T. Smith (eds), *Recent Advances in the Psychology of Language: Formal and Experimental Approaches*, pp. 347–60. Boston, MA:Springer. DOI: 10.1007/978-1-4684-2532-1_19

Byrne, Richard W., Erica A. Cartmill, Emilie Genty, Kirsty E. Graham, Catherine Hobaiter, and Joanne E. Tanner. (2017). 'Great ape gestures: intentional communication with a rich set of innate signals', *Animal Cognition*, 20/4: 755–69. DOI: 10.1007/s10071-017-1096-4

Calbris, Geneviève. (2008). 'From left to right ... Coverbal gestures and their symbolic use of space'. Alan Cienki, and Cornelia Müller (eds), *Metaphor and Gesture*, pp. 27–53. Amsterdam: John Benjamins. DOI: 10.1075/gs.3.05cal

Calbris, Geneviève. (2011). *Elements of Meaning in Gesture*. (M. M. Copple, Tran.). Amsterdam: John Benjamins. DOI: 10.1075/gs.5

Campana, Ellen, Jessica Mumford, Cristóbal Martínez, Stjepan Rajko, Todd Ingalls, Lisa Tolentino, and Harvey Thornburg. (2011). 'Handjabber: Exploring metaphoric gesture and non-verbal communication via an interactive art installation'. Gale Stam and Mika Ishino (eds), *Intergrating Gestures*, pp. 355–64. Amsterdam: John Benjamins. DOI: 10.1075/gs.4.32cam

Capirci, Olga, Maria Cristina Caselli, and Virginia Volterra. (2021). 'Interaction among modalities and within development'. Aliyah Morgenstern, and Susan Goldin-Meadow (eds), *Gesture in Language*, pp. 113–34. Washington DC/Berlin:APA/De Gruyter. DOI: 10.1515/9783110567526-005

Casasanto, Daniel, and Kyle Jasmin. (2012). 'The hands of time: Temporal gestures in English speakers', *Cognitive Linguistics*, 23/4: 643–74. DOI: 10.1515/cog-2012-0020

Casey, Shannon, and Karen Emmorey. (2009). 'Co-speech gesture in bimodal bilinguals', *Language and Cognitive Processes*, 24/2: 290–312. DOI: 10.1080/01690960801916188

Casey, Shannon, Karen Emmorey, and Heather Larrabee. (2012). 'The effects of learning American Sign Language on co-speech gesture', *Bilingualism*, 15/4: 677–86. DOI: 10.1017/S1366728911000575

Cassell, Justine. (2007). 'Body language: lessons from the near-human'. Jessica Riskin (ed.), *Genesis Redux: Essays in the History and Philosophy of Artificial Life*, pp. 346–74. Chicago:University of Chicago Press.

Chen, Jenn Yeu, and Padraig G. O'Seaghdha. (2013). 'Do Mandarin and English speakers think about time differently? Review of existing evidence and some new data', *Journal of Chinese Linguistics*, 41/2: 338–58.

Choi, Boin, Ran Wei, and Meredith L. Rowe. (2021). 'Show, give, and point gestures across infancy differentially predict language development', *Developmental Psychology*, 57/6: 851–62. DOI: 10.1037/dev0001195

Chui, Kawai. (2011). 'Conceptual metaphors in gesture', *Cognitive Linguistics*, 22/3. DOI: 10.1515/cogl.2011.017

Cienki, Alan. (2008). 'Why study metaphor and gesture?'. Alan Cienki and Cornelia Müller (eds), *Metaphor and Gesture*, pp. 5–25. Amsterdam:John Benjamins. DOI: 10.1075/gs.3.04cie

Cienki, Alan J. (ed.). (2024). *The Cambridge Handbook of Gesture Studies*. Cambridge/New York: Cambridge University Press.

Cienki, Alan, and Cornelia Müller. (2008). 'Metaphor, gesture, and thought'. Raymond W. Gibbs, Jr. (ed.), *The Cambridge Handbook of Metaphor and Thought*, pp. 483–501. Cambridge: Cambridge University Press. DOI: 10.1017/CBO9780511816802.029

Cirillo, Letizia. (2019). 'The pragmatics of air quotes in English academic presentations', *Journal of Pragmatics*, 142: 1–15. DOI: 10.1016/j.pragma.2018.12.022

Clark, Eve V., and Barbara F. Kelly. (2021). 'Constructing a system of communication with gestures and words'. Aliyah Morgenstern and Susan Goldin-Meadow (eds), *Gesture in Language*, pp. 137–56. Washington DC/Berlin:APA/De Gruyter. DOI: 10.1515/9783110567526-006

Clough, Sharice, and Melissa C. Duff. (2020). 'The role of gesture in communication and cognition: Implications for understanding and treating neurogenic communication disorders', *Frontiers in Human Neuroscience*, 14: 323. DOI: 10.3389/fnhum.2020.00323

Cohen, Akiba A. (1977). 'The communicative functions of hand Illustrators', *Journal of Communication*, 27/4: 54–63. DOI: 10.1111/j.1460-2466.1977.tb01856.x

Cohn, Neil, and Sean Ehly. (2016). 'The vocabulary of manga: Visual morphology in dialects of Japanese Visual Language', *Journal of Pragmatics*, 92: 17–29. DOI: 10.1016/j.pragma.2015.11.008

Cohn, Neil, and Joost Schilperoord. (2024). *A Multimodal Language Faculty: A Cognitive Framework for Human Communication*. London/New York: Bloomsbury Academic.

Colletta, Jean-Marc. (2004). *Le développement de la parole chez l'enfant âgé de 6 à 11 ans: corps, langage et cognition*. Psychologie et sciences humaines. Sprimont: Mardaga.

Colonnesi, Cristina, Geert Jan J. M. Stams, Irene Koster, and Marc J. Noom. (2010). 'The relation between pointing and language development: A meta-analysis', *Developmental Review*, 30/4: 352–66. DOI: 10.1016/j.dr.2010.10.001

Cook, Susan Wagner, Terina KuangYi Yip, and Susan Goldin-Meadow. (2010). 'Gesturing makes memories that last', *Journal of Memory and Language*, 63/4: 465–75. DOI: 10.1016/j.jml.2010.07.002

Cooperrider, Kensy. (2017). 'Foreground gesture, background gesture', *Gesture*, 16/2: 176–202. DOI: 10.1075/gest.16.2.02coo

Cooperrider, Kensy. (2020). 'Fifteen ways of looking at a pointing gesture' (preprint). *PsyArXiv*. DOI: 10.31234/osf.io/2vxft

Cooperrider, Kensy, Natasha Abner, and Susan Goldin-Meadow. (2018a). 'The palm-up puzzle: Meanings and origins of a widespread form in gesture and sign', *Frontiers in Communication*, 3. Retrieved from PDF. DOI: 10.3389/fcomm.2018.00023

Cooperrider, Kensy, James Slotta, and Rafael Núñez. (2018b). 'The preference for pointing with the hand is not universal', *Cognitive Science*, 42/4: 1375–90. DOI: 10.1111/cogs.12585

Corballis, Michael C. (2013). 'Gesture as precursor to speech in evolution'. Cornelia Müller, Alan Cienki, Ellen Fricke, Silva Ladewig, David McNeill, and Sedinha Tessendorf (eds), *Body—Language—Communication: An International Handbook on Multimodality in Human Interaction*, Vol. 1, pp. 466–80. Berlin/Boston: De Gruyter. DOI: 10.1515/9783110261318

Cravotta, Alice, M. Grazia Busà, and Pilar Prieto. (2019). 'Effects of encouraging the use of gestures on speech', *Journal of Speech, Language, and Hearing Research*, 62/9: 3204–19. DOI: 10.1044/2019_JSLHR-S-18-0493

Darwin, Charles. (1872). *The Expression of the Emotions in Man and Animals*. London: John Murray.

Demir, Özlem Ece, Susan C. Levine, and Susan Goldin-Meadow. (2015). 'A tale of two hands: children's early gesture use in narrative production predicts later narrative structure in speech', *Journal of Child Language*, 42/3: 662–81. DOI: 10.1017/S0305000914000415

Dobrogaev, Sergej M. (1929). 'Ucnenie o reflekse v problemakh iazykovedeniia [Observations on reflexes and issues in language study]', *Iazykovedenie i materializm*, 105–73.

Efron, David. (1941). *Gesture, Race and Culture; A Tentative Study of the Spatio-temporal and 'Linguistic' Aspects of the Gestural Behavior of Eastern Jews and Southern Italians in New York City, Living under Similar as well as Different Environmental Conditions*. The Hague: Mouton.

Ekman, Paul, and Wallace V. Friesen. (1969). 'The repertiore of nonverbal behaviour: Categories, origins, usage, and coding', *Semiotica*, 1: 49–98. DOI: 10.1515/semi.1969.1.1.49

Ekman, Paul, and Wallace V. Friesen. (1972). 'Hand movements', *Journal of Communication*, 22/4: 353–74. DOI: 10.1111/j.1460-2466.1972.tb00163.x

ELAN (Version 6.8) [Computer software]. (2024). Nijmegen: Max Planck Institute for Psycholinguistics, The Language Archive.

Emmorey, Karen. (1999). 'Do signers gesture?'. Lynn Messing and Ruth Campbell (eds), *Gesture, Speech, and Sign*, pp. 133–58. Oxford: Oxford University Press. DOI: 10.1093/acprof:oso/9780198524519.003.0008

Emmorey, Karen. (2005). 'Sign languages are problematic for a gestural origins theory of language evolution', *Behavioral and Brain Sciences*, 28/2: 130–31. DOI: 10.1017/S0140525X05270036

Emmorey, Karen, Helsa B. Borinstein, Robin Thompson, and Tamar H. Gollan. (2008a). 'Bimodal bilingualism', *Bilingualism: Language and Cognition*, 11/1: 43–61. DOI: 10.1017/S1366728907003203

Emmorey, Karen, R. Thompson, and R. Colvin. (2008b). 'Eye gaze during comprehension of American Sign Language by native and beginning signers', *Journal of Deaf Studies and Deaf Education*, 14/2: 237–43. DOI: 10.1093/deafed/enn037

Enfield, N. J. (2001). '"Lip-pointing": A discussion of form and function with reference to data from Laos', *Gesture*, 1/2: 185–211. DOI: https://doi.org/10.1075/gest.1.2.06enf

Farnell, Brenda Margaret. (1995). *Do you see what I mean?: Plains Indian Sign Talk and the Embodiment of Action*. Austin: University of Texas Press.

Fenlon, Jordan, Kensy Cooperrider, Jon Keane, Diane Brentari, and Susan Goldin-Meadow. (2019). 'Comparing sign language and gesture: Insights from pointing', *Glossa*, 4/1. DOI: 10.5334/gjgl.499

Feyereisen, Pierre, Michèle Van de Wiele, and Fabienne Dubois. (1988). 'The meaning of gestures: What can be understood without speech?', *Cahiers de Psychologie Cognitive/Current Psychology of Cognition*, 8/1: 3–25.

Fitch, W. Tecumseh, Ludwig Huber, and Thomas Bugnyar. (2010). 'Social cognition and the evolution of language: Constructing cognitive phylogenies', *Neuron*, 65: 795–814.

de Fornel, Michel. (1992). 'The return gesture: Some remarks on context, inference, and iconic gesture'. Peter Auer and Aldo Di Luzio (eds), *The Contextualization of Language*, pp. 159–76. Amsterdam/Philadelphia: John Benjamins.

Forrester, Gillian S., and Alina Rodriguez. (2015). 'Slip of the tongue: Implications for evolution and language development', *Cognition*, 141: 103–11. DOI: 10.1016/j.cognition.2015.04.012

Franklin, Amy. (2007). 'Liar, liar, hands on fire: What gesture-speech asynchrony reveals about thinking' (PhD Thesis). The University of Chicago.

Freestone, Peta M., Jessica Kruk, and Lauren Gawne. (2023). 'From Star Trek to The Hunger Games: Emblem gestures in science fiction and their uptake in popular culture', *Linguistic Vanguards*, 9/s3: 257–66. DOI: https://doi.org/10.1515/lingvan-2023-0006

Frey, Scott H. (2008). 'Tool use, communicative gesture and cerebral asymmetries in the modern human brain', *Philosophical Transactions of the Royal Society B: Biological Sciences*, 363/1499: 1951–57. DOI: 10.1098/rstb.2008.0008

de la Fuente, Juanma, Julio Santiago, Antonio Román, Cristina Dumitrache, and Daniel Casasanto. (2014). 'When you think about it, your past is in front of you: How culture shapes spatial conceptions of time', *Psychological Science*, 25/9: 1682–90. DOI: 10.1177/0956797614534695

Furuyama, Nobuhiro. (2000). 'Gestural interactions between the instructor and the learner in origmi instructions'. David McNeill (ed.), *Language and Gesture: Window into Thought and Action*, pp. 99–117. Cambridge:Cambridge University Press.

Gaby, Alice. (2012). 'The Thaayorre think of time like they talk of space', *Frontiers in Psychology*, 3: 1–8. DOI: 10.3389/fpsyg.2012.00300

Gawne, Lauren. (2018). 'Contexts of use of a rotated palms gesture among Syuba (Kagate) speakers in Nepal', *Gesture*, 17/1: 37–64. DOI: 10.1075/gest.00010.gaw

Gawne, Lauren. (2021). '"Away" gestures associated with negative expressions in narrative discourse in Syuba (Kagate, Nepal) speakers', *Semiotica*, 2021/239: 37–59. DOI: 10.1515/sem-2017-0163

Gawne, Lauren, and Kensy Cooperrider. (2024). 'Emblems: Meaning at the interface of language and gesture', *Glossa*, 9/1: 1–34. DOI: 10.16995/glossa.9705

Gawne, Lauren, and Gretchen McCulloch. (2019). 'Emoji as digital gestures', *Language@Internet*, 17/2.

Gawne, Lauren, Barbara Kelly, and Annie Unger. (2010). 'Gesture categorisation and understanding speaker attention to gesture'. Yvonne Treis and Rik De Busser (eds), *Selected Papers from the 2009 Conference of the Australian Linguistic Society*. Melbourne: La Trobe University.

Geladó, Sandra, Isabel Gómez-Ruiz, and Faustino Diéguez-Vide. (2022). 'Gestures analysis during a picture description task: Capacity to discriminate between healthy controls, mild cognitive impairment, and Alzheimer's disease', *Journal of Neurolinguistics*, 61: 101038. DOI: 10.1016/j.jneuroling.2021.101038

Göksun, Tilbe, Demet Özer, and Seda Akbıyık. (2021). 'Gesture in the aging brain'. Aliyah Morgenstern and Susan Goldin-Meadow (eds), *Gesture in Language*, pp. 269–94. Washington DC/Berlin: APA/De Gruyter. DOI: 10.1515/9783110567526-011

Goldin-Meadow, Susan. (2023). *Thinking with your Hands: The Surprising Science behind how Gestures Shape our Thoughts*. New York: Basic Books.

Goldin-Meadow, Susan, and Catherine Momeni Sandhofer. (1999). 'Gestures convey substantive information about a child's thoughts to ordinary listeners', *Developmental Science*, 2/1: 67–74. DOI: 10.1111/1467-7687.00056

Goldin-Meadow, Susan, and Carolyn Mylander. (1990). 'The role of parental input in the development of a morphological system', *Journal of Child Language*, 17/3: 527–63. DOI: 10.1017/S0305000900010874

Goldin-Meadow, Susan, and Jody Saltzman. (2000). 'The cultural bounds of maternal accommodation: How Chinese and American mothers communicate with deaf and hearing children', *Psychological Science*, 11/4: 307–14. DOI: 10.1111/1467-9280.00261

Goldin-Meadow, Susan, Carolyn Mylander, Jill de Villiers, Elizabeth Bates, and Virginia Volterra. (1984). 'Gestural communication in deaf children: The effects and noneffects of parental input on early language development', *Monographs of the Society for Research in Child Development*, 49/3/4: 1–151. DOI: 10.2307/1165838

Goldin-Meadow, Susan, Howard Nusbaum, Spencer D. Kelly, and Susan Wagner. (2001). 'Explaining math: Gesturing lightens the load', *Psychological Science*, 12/6: 516–22. DOI: 10.1111/1467-9280.00395

Goodwin, Charles. (1980). 'Restarts, pauses, and the achievement of a state of mutual gaze at turn-beginning', *Sociological Inquiry*, 50/3–4: 272–302. DOI: 10.1111/j.1475-682X.1980.tb00023.x

Goodwin, Charles. (2000). 'Gesture, aphasia and interaction'. David McNeill (ed.), *Language and Gesture: Window into Thought and Action*, pp. 84–98. Cambridge: Cambridge University Press.

Goodwin, Charles. (2003). 'Pointing as situated practice'. Sotaro Kita (ed.), *Pointing: Where Language, Culture, and Cognition Meet*, pp. 217–41. Mahwah, NJ: L. Erlbaum Associates.

Goodwin, Charles. (2007). 'Environmentally coupled gestures'. Susan D. Duncan, Justine Cassell and Elena T. Levy (eds), *Gesture and the Dynamic Dimensions of Language: Essays in honor of David McNeill*, pp. 195–212. Amsterdam: John Benjamins.

Graham, Jean Ann, and Simon Heywood. (1975). 'The effects of elimination of hand gestures and of verbal codability on speech performance', *European Journal of Social Psychology*, 5/2: 159–95. DOI: https://doi.org/10.1002/ejsp.2420050204graha

Graham, Kirsty E., and Catherine Hobaiter. (2023). 'Towards a great ape dictionary: Inexperienced humans understand common nonhuman ape gestures', *PLOS Biology*, 21/1: e3001939. DOI: 10.1371/journal.pbio.3001939

Green, Jennifer, and David P. Wilkins. (2014). 'With or without speech: Arandic Sign Language from Central Australia', *Australian Journal of Linguistics*, 34/2: 234–61. DOI: 10.1080/07268602.2014.887407

Grenoble, Lenore A., Martina Martinović, and Rebekah Baglini. (2014). 'Verbal gestures in Wolof'. Ruth Kramer, Elizabeth C. Zsiga, and One Tlale Boyer (eds), *Selected Proceedings of the 44th annual conference on African linguistics*, pp. 110–21. Somerville, MA: Cascadilla Press.

Gu, Yan. (2018). *Chinese Hands of Time: The Effects of Language and Culture on Temporal Gestures and Spatio-temporal Reasoning.* Utrecht: LOT.

Gullberg, Marianne. (1998). *Gesture as a Communication Strategy in Second Language Discourse.* Lund: Lund University Press.

Gullberg, Marianne. (2009). 'Reconstructing verb meaning in a second language: How English speakers of L2 Dutch talk and gesture about placement', *Annual Review of Cognitive Linguistics*, 7: 221–44. DOI: 10.1075/arcl.7.09gul

Gullberg, Marianne. (2021). 'Bimodal convergence: How languages interact in multicompetent language users' speech and gestures'. Aliyah Morgenstern and Susan Goldin-Meadow (eds), *Gesture in Language*, pp. 317–34. Washington DC/Berlin: APA/De Gruyter. DOI: 10.1515/9783110567526-013

Gullberg, Marianne, and Kenneth Holmqvist. (2006). 'What speakers do and what addressees look at: Visual attention to gestures in human interaction live and on video', *Pragmatics & Cognition*, 14/1: 53–82. DOI: 10.1075/pc.14.1.05gul

Hadar, Uri. (1989). 'Two types of gesture and their role in speech production', *Journal of Language and Social Psychology*, 8/3–4: 221–28. DOI: 10.1177/0261927X8983004

Hahamy, Avital, Scott N. Macdonald, Fiona van den Heiligenberg, Paullina Kieliba, Uzay Emir, Rafael Malach, Heidi Johansen-Berg, et al. (2017). 'Representation of multiple body parts in the missing-hand territory of congenital one-handers', *Current Biology*, 27/9: 1350–55. DOI: 10.1016/j.cub.2017.03.053

Hammarström, Harald, Robert Forkel, Martin Haspelmath, and Sebastian Bank. (2023). 'glottolog/glottolog: Glottolog database 4.8'. Zenodo. DOI: 10.5281/ZENODO.8131084

Harness Goodwin, Marjorie, and Charles Goodwin. (1986). 'Gesture and coparticipation in the activity of searching for a word', *Semiotica*, 62/1–2. DOI: 10.1515/semi.1986.62.1-2.51

Harrison, Simon. (2010). 'Evidence for node and scope of negation in coverbal gesture', *Gesture*, 10/1: 29–51. DOI: 10.1075/gest.10.1.03har

Harrison, Simon. (2014). 'Gestures in industrial settings'. Cornelia Müller, Alan J. Cienki, Ellen Fricke, Silva Ladewig, David McNeill, and Sedinha Tessendorf (eds), *Body—Language—Communication: An International Handbook on Multimodality in Human Communication*, Vol. 2, pp. 1147–53. Berlin:de Gruyter.

Hasegawa, Dai, Justine Cassell, and Kenji Araki. (2010). 'The role of embodiment and perspective in direction-giving systems'. *Dialog with Robots: Papers from the AAAI Fall Symposium*, pp. 26–31. Association for the Advancement of Artificial Intelligence.

Haviland, John B. (2000). 'Pointing, gesture spaces, and mental maps'. David McNeill (ed.), *Language and Gesture: Window into Thought and Action*, pp. 13–46. Cambridge:Cambridge University Press.

Healy, Christina. (2012). 'Pointing to show agreement', *Semiotica*, 2012/192: 175–96. DOI: 10.1515/sem-2012-0073

Heath, Christian. (1992). 'Gesture's discreet tasks: Multiple relevancies in visual conduct and in the contextualisation of language'. Peter Auer and Aldo Di Luzio (eds), *The Contextualization of Language*, pp. 101–27. Amsterdam/Philadelphia: John Benjamins.

Hewes, Gordon W. (1974). 'Gesture language in culture contact', *Sign Language Studies*, 4/1: 1–34. DOI: 10.1353/sls.1974.0010

Hobaiter, Catherine. (2020). 'Gestural communication in the great apes: Tracing the origins of l anguage'. Jane Goodall, Lydia M. Hopper, and Stephen R. Ross (eds), *Chimpanzees in Context: A Comparative Perspective on Chimpanzee Behavior, Cognition, Conservation, and Welfare*, pp. 233–59. Chicago:University of Chicago Press. DOI: 10.7208/chicago/9780226728032.003.0010

Hobaiter, Catherine, and Richard W. Byrne. (2011a). 'The gestural repertoire of the wild chimpanzee', *Animal Cognition*, 14/5: 745–67. DOI: 10.1007/s10071-011-0409-2

Hobaiter, Catherine, and Richard W. Byrne. (2011b). 'Serial gesturing by wild chimpanzees: its nature and function for communication', *Animal Cognition*, 14/6: 827–38. DOI: 10.1007/s10071-011-0416-3

Hobaiter, Catherine, and Richard W. Byrne. (2014). 'The Meanings of Chimpanzee Gestures', *Current Biology*, 24/14: 1596–600. DOI: 10.1016/j.cub.2014.05.066

Hobaiter, Catherine, David A. Leavens, and Richard W. Byrne. (2014). 'Deictic gesturing in wild chimpanzees (Pan troglodytes)? Some possible cases', *Journal of Comparative Psychology*, 128/1: 82–87. DOI: 10.1037/a0033757

Hockett, Charles F. (1960). 'The origin of speech', *Scientific American*, 203/3: 88–97. DOI: 10.1038/scientificamerican0960-88

Hodge, Gabrielle, and Trevor Johnston. (2014). 'Points, depictions, gestures and enactment: Partly lexical and non-lexical signs as core elements of single clause-like units in Auslan (Australian Sign Language)', *Australian Journal of Linguistics*, 34/2: 262–91. DOI: 10.1080/07268602.2014.887408

Hoetjes, Marieke, Emiel Krahmer, and Marc Swerts. (2014). 'Does our speech change when we cannot gesture?', *Speech Communication*, 57: 257–67. DOI: 10.1016/j.specom.2013.06.007

Holle, Henning, Thomas C. Gunter, Shirley-Ann Rüschemeyer, Andreas Hennenlotter, and Marco Iacoboni. (2008). 'Neural correlates of the processing of co-speech gestures', *NeuroImage*, 39/4: 2010–24. DOI: 10.1016/j.neuroimage.2007.10.055

Hostetter, Autumn B., and Martha W. Alibali. (2008). 'Visible embodiment: Gestures as simulated action', *Psychonomic Bulletin & Review*, 15/3: 495–514. DOI: 10.3758/PBR.15.3.495

Hostetter, Autumn B., and Martha W. Alibali. (2019). 'Gesture as simulated action: Revisiting the framework', *Psychonomic Bulletin & Review*, 26/3: 721–52. DOI: 10.3758/s13423-018-1548-0

Hostetter, Autumn B., Martha W. Alibali, and Sheree M. Schrager. (2011). 'If you don't already know, I'm certainly not going to show you!: Motivation to communicate affects gesture production'. Gale Stam and Mika Ishino (eds), *Integrating Gestures: The Interdisciplinary Nature of Gesture*, Vol. 4, pp. 61–74. Amsterdam: John Benjamins. DOI: 10.1075/gs.4.06hos

Hsieh, Jessica. (2012). *The Alignment of Gestures and Intonation in Pwo Karen* (Senior essay). Yale University.

Iverson, Jana M., and Esther Thelen. (1999). 'Hand, mouth and brain: The dynamic emergence of speech and gesture', *Journal of Consciousness Studies*, 6/11–12: 19–40.

Iverson, Jana M., Olga Capirci, and M. Cristina Caselli. (1994). 'From communication to language in two modalities', *Cognitive Development*, 9/1: 23–43. DOI: 10.1016/0885-2014(94)90018-3

Iverson, Jana M., Olga Capirci, Emiddia Longobardi, and M. Cristina Caselli. (1999). 'Gesturing in mother–child interactions', *Cognitive Development*, 14/1: 57–75. DOI: 10.1016/S0885-2014(99)80018-5

Jarmołowicz-Nowikow, Ewa. (2015). 'How Poles indicate people and objects, and what they think of certain forms of pointing gestures', *Lingua Posnaniensis*, 56/1: 85–95. DOI: 10.2478/linpo-2014-0005

Johnston, J. Cyne, Andrée Durieux-Smith, and Kathleen Bloom. (2005). 'Teaching gestural signs to infants to advance child development: A review of the evidence', *First Language*, 25/2: 235–51. DOI: 10.1177/0142723705050340

de Jorio, Andrea. (1832). *Gesture in Naples and Gesture in Classical Antiquity: A Translation of La mimica degli antichi investigata nel gestire napoletano, Gestural Expression of the Ancients in the Light of Neapolitan Gesturing*. (A. Kendon, Tran.). Indianapolis: Indiana University Press.

Kaas, Jon H. (2004). 'Evolution of somatosensory and motor cortex in primates', *The Anatomical Record*, 281A/1: 1148–56. DOI: 10.1002/ar.a.20120

Kelly, Barbara F. (2014). 'Temporal synchrony in early multi-modal communication'. Inbal Arnon, Marisa Casillas, Chigusa Kurumada, and Bruno Estigarribia (eds), *Language in Interaction: Studies in Honor of Eve V. Clark*, Vol. 12, pp. 117–38. Amsterdam: John Benjamins. DOI: 10.1075/tilar.12.11kel

Kelly, Spencer D. (2017). 'Exploring the boundaries of gesture-speech integration during language comprehension'. R. Breckinridge Church, Martha W. Alibali, and Spencer D. Kelly (eds), *Why Gesture?: How the Hands Function in Speaking, Thinking and Communicating*, pp. 243–65. Amsterdam: John Benjamins. DOI: 10.1075/gs.7.12kel

Kendon, Adam. (1980). 'Gesticulation and speech: two aspects of the process of utterance'. Mary Ritchie, Key (ed.), *The Relationship of Verbal and Nonverbal Communication*, pp. 207–27. Mouton: The Hague/New York.

Kendon, Adam. (1981). 'Geography of gesture', *Semiotica*, 37/2: 129–63.

Kendon, Adam. (1983). 'Gesture and speech: how they interact'. J. M. Wiemann and R. P. Harrison (eds), *Nonverbal Interaction*, pp. 13–45. Beverly Hills: Sage.

Kendon, Adam. (1988). *Sign Languages of Aboriginal Australia. Cultural, Semiotic and Communicative Perspectives*. Cambridge: Cambridge University Press.

Kendon, Adam. (2004). *Gesture: Visible Action as Utterance*. Cambridge: Cambridge University Press.

Kendon, Adam, and Laura Versante. (2003). 'Pointing by hand in "Neapolitan"'. Sotaro Kita (ed.), *Pointing: Where Language, Culture, and Cognition Meet*, pp. 109–37. Mahwah, NJ: L. Erlbaum Associates.

Kendrick, Kobin H., Judith Holler, and Stephen C. Levinson. (2023). 'Turn-taking in human face-to-face interaction is multimodal: gaze direction and manual gestures aid the coordination of turn transitions', *Philosophical Transactions of the Royal Society B: Biological Sciences*, 378/1875: 20210473. DOI: 10.1098/rstb.2021.0473

Kersken, Verena, Juan-Carlos Gómez, Ulf Liszkowski, Adrian Soldati, and Catherine Hobaiter. (2019). 'A gestural repertoire of 1- to 2-year-old human children: in search of the ape gestures', *Animal Cognition*, 22/4: 577–95. DOI: 10.1007/s10071-018-1213-z

Kettner, Viktoria A., and Jeremy I. M. Carpendale. (2013). 'Developing gestures for *no* and *yes*: Head shaking and nodding in infancy', *Gesture*, 13/2: 193–209. DOI: 10.1075/gest.13.2.04ket

Kirk, Elizabeth, Neil Howlett, Karen J. Pine, and Ben (C) Fletcher. (2013). 'To sign or not to sign? The impact of encouraging infants to gesture on infant language and maternal mind-mindedness', *Child Development*, 84/2: 574–90. DOI: 10.1111/j.1467-8624.2012.01874.x

Kısa, Yağmur Deniz. (2022). 'A communicative account of gesturing when speaking is difficult' (PhD Thesis). The University of Chicago.

Kita, Sotaro (ed.). (2003). *Pointing: Where Language, Culture, and Cognition Meet*. Mahwah, NJ: L. Erlbaum Associates.

Kita, Sotaro. (2009). 'Cross-cultural variation of speech-accompanying gesture: A review', *Language and Cognitive Processes*, 24/2: 145–67. DOI: 10.1080/01690960802586188

Kita, Sotaro, and James Essegbey. (2001). 'Pointing left in Ghana: How a taboo on the use of the left hand influences gestural practice', *Gesture*, 1/1: 73–95. DOI: 10.1075/gest.1.1.06kit

Kita, Sotaro, and Sachiko Ide. (2007). 'Nodding, aizuchi, and final particles in Japanese conversation: How conversation reflects the ideology of communication and social relationships', *Journal of Pragmatics*, 39/7: 1242–54. DOI: 10.1016/j.pragma.2007.02.009

Kita, Sotaro, and Asli Özyürek. (2003). 'What does cross-linguistic variation in semantic coordination of speech and gesture reveal? Evidence for an interface representation of spatial thinking and speaking', *Journal of Memory and Language*, 48: 16–32. DOI: https://doi.org/10.1016/S0749-596X(02)00505-3

Kita, Sotaro, Ingeborg Van Gijn, and Harry Van Der Hulst. (1998). 'Movement phases in signs and co-speech gestures, and their transcription by human coders'. Ipke Wachsmuth and Martin Fröhlich (eds), *Gesture and Sign Language in Human-Computer Interaction*, Vol. 1371, pp. 23–35. Berlin/Heidelberg:Springer. DOI: 10.1007/BFb0052986

Kita, Sotaro, Asli Özyürek, Shanley Allen, Amanda Brown, Reyhan Furman, and Tomoko Ishizuka. (2007). 'Relations between syntactic encoding and co-speech gestures: Implications for a model of speech and gesture production', *Language and Cognitive Processes*, 22/8: 1212–36. DOI: 10.1080/01690960701461426

Kita, Sotaro, Martha W. Alibali, and Mingyuan Chu. (2017). 'How do gestures influence thinking and speaking? The gesture-for-conceptualization hypothesis.', *Psychological Review*, 124/3: 245–66. DOI: 10.1037/rev0000059

Krajcik, Chelsea Lee. (2020). 'Exploring multilingualism in Senegal: a multimodal approach to the expression of caused motion' (PhD Thesis). SOAS University of London. DOI: 10.25501/SOAS.00037844

Krauss, Robert M., Yihsui Chen, and Rebecca F. Gottesman. (2000). 'Lexical gestures and lexical access: A process model'. David McNeill (ed.), *Language and Gesture: Window into Thought and Action*, pp. 261–83. Cambridge:Cambridge University Press.

Kroenke, Klaus-Martin, Indra Kraft, Frank Regenbrecht, and Hellmuth Obrig. (2013). 'Lexical learning in mild aphasia: Gesture benefit depends on patholinguistic profile and lesion pattern', *Cortex*, 49/10: 2637–49. DOI: 10.1016/j.cortex.2013.07.012

Lakoff, George, and Mark Johnson. (1980). *Metaphors We Live by*. Chicago: University of Chicago Press.

Laparle, Schuyler. (2022). 'The shape of discourse: How gesture structures conversation' (PhD Thesis). University of California, Berkeley, Berkeley. DOI: 10.13140/RG.2.2.22164.17283

Le Guen, Olivier, and Lorena Ildefonsa Pool Balam. (2012). 'No metaphorical timeline in gesture and cognition among Yucatec Mayas', *Frontiers in Psychology*, 3. DOI: 10.3389/fpsyg.2012.00271

Lempert, Michael. (2011). 'Barack Obama, being sharp: Indexical order in the pragmatics of precision-grip gesture', *Gesture*, 11/3: 241–70. DOI: 10.1075/gest.11.3.01lem

Levelt, Willem J. M. (1989). *Speaking: From Intention to Articulation*. Cambridge, MA: MIT Press.

Levinson, Stephen C. (1997). 'Language and cognition: The cognitive consequences of spatial description in Guugu Yimithirr', *Journal of Linguistic Anthropology*, 7/1: 98–131. DOI: 10.1525/jlin.1997.7.1.98

Levinson, Stephen C. (2003). *Space in Language and Cognition: Explorations in Cognitive Diversity*. Cambridge: Cambridge University Press. DOI: 10.1017/CBO9780511613609

Levinson, Stephen C., and Asifa Majid. (2013). 'The island of time: Yélî Dnye, the language of Rossel Island', *Frontiers in Psychology*, 4. DOI: 10.3389/fpsyg.2013.00061

Levinson, Stephen C., and David Wilkins (eds). (2006). *Grammars of Space: Explorations in Cognitive Diversity*. Cambridge/New York: Cambridge University Press.

Li, Heng. (2023). 'Personality in your hands: How extraversion traits influence preference for pointing in Chinese people', *Australian Journal of Linguistics*, 43/2: 121–36. DOI: 10.1080/07268602.2023.2226094

Lickiss, Karen P., and A. Rodney Wellens. (1978). 'Effects of visual accessibility and hand restraint on fluency of gesticulator and effectiveness of message', *Perceptual and Motor Skills*, 46/3: 925–26. DOI: 10.2466/pms.1978.46.3.925

Lillo-Martin, Diane, Ronice Müller De Quadros, and Deborah Chen Pichler. (2016). 'The development of bimodal bilingualism: Implications for linguistic theory', *Linguistic Approaches to Bilingualism*, 6/6: 719–55. DOI: 10.1075/lab.6.6.01lil

Liszkowski, Ulf. (2008). 'Before L1: A differentiated perspective on infant gestures', *Gesture*, 8/2: 180–96. DOI: 10.1075/gest.8.2.04lis

Liszkowski, Ulf, Penny Brown, Tara Callaghan, Akira Takada, and Conny de Vos. (2012). 'A prelinguistic gestural universal of human communication', *Cognitive Science*, 36/4: 698–713. DOI: 10.1111/j.1551-6709.2011.01228.x

Loehr, Daniel P. (2012). 'Temporal, structural, and pragmatic synchrony between intonation and gesture', *Laboratory Phonology*, 3/1. DOI: 10.1515/lp-2012-0006

Lüke, Carina, Angela Grimminger, Katharina J. Rohlfing, Ulf Liszkowski, and Ute Ritterfeld. (2017). 'In infants' hands: Identification of preverbal infants at risk for primary language delay', *Child Development*, 88/2: 484–92. DOI: 10.1111/cdev.12610

McCafferty, Steven G., and Gale Stam. (2008). *Gesture: Second Language Acquistion and Classroom Research*. Routledge. DOI: 10.4324/9780203866993

McCulloch, Gretchen. (2019). *Because Internet: Understanding the New Rules of Language*. New York: Riverhead Books.

McKern, Nicola, Nicole Dargue, and Naomi Sweller. (2023). 'Comparing gesture frequency between autistic and neurotypical individuals: A systematic review and meta-analysis', Psychological Bulletin. US: American Psychological Association. DOI: 10.1037/bul0000408

MacLean, Evan L., Christopher Krupenye, and Brian Hare. (2014). 'Dogs (Canis familiaris) account for body orientation but not visual barriers when responding to pointing gestures', *Journal of Comparative Psychology*, 128/3: 285–97. DOI: 10.1037/a0035742

McNeill, David. (1985). 'So you think gestures are nonverbal?', *Psychological Review*, 92/3: 350–71.

McNeill, David. (1992). *Hand and Mind: What Gestures Reveal about Thought*. Chicago: The University of Chicago Press.

McNeill, David. (2005). *Gesture and Thought*. Chicago: University of Chicago Press.

McNeill, David. (2012). *How Language Began*. Cambridge: Cambridge University Press.

McNeill, David, and Susan Duncan. (2000). 'Growth points in thinking-for-speaking'. David McNeill (ed.), *Language and Gesture: Window into Thought and Action*, pp. 141–61. Cambridge:Cambridge University Press.

McNeill, David, and Elena Levy. (1982). 'Conceptual representations in language activity and gesture'. Robert J. Jarvella and Wolfgang Klein (eds), *Speech, Place, and Action: Studies in Deixis and Related Topics*, pp. 271–96. Chichester: Wiley.

McNeill, David, Justine Cassell, and Karl-Eric McCullough. (1994). 'Communicative effects of speech-mismatched gestures', *Research on Language and Social Interation*, 27/3: 223–37.

Mallery, Garrick. (1881). *Sign Language among North American Indians: Compared with That among Other Peoples and Deaf-Mutes*. The Hague: Mouton.

Marschark, Marc. (1994). 'Gesture and sign', *Applied Psycholinguistics*, 15/2: 209–36. DOI: 10.1017/S0142716400005336

Masataka, Nobuo. (1995). 'The relation between index-finger extension and the acoustic quality of cooing in three-month-old infants', *Journal of Child Language*, 22/2: 247–57. DOI: 10.1017/S0305000900009776

Masataka, Nobuo. (2003). 'From index-finger extension to index-finger pointing: ontogenesis of pointing in preverbal infants'. Sotaro Kita (ed.), *Pointing: where Language, Culture, and Cognition Meet*, pp. 69–84. Mahwah, NJ: L. Erlbaum Associates.

Mashal, Nira, Michael Andric, and Steven Small. (2012). 'Motor and nonmotor language representations in the brain'. Miriam Faust (ed.), *The Handbook of the Neuropsychology of Language*, pp. 276–93. Oxford: Wiley-Blackwell. DOI: 10.1002/9781118432501.ch14

Mayberry, Rachel I., and Joselynne Jaques. (2000). 'Gesture production during stuttered speech: Insight into the nature of gesture-speech intergration'. David McNeill (ed.), *Language and Gesture: Window into Thought and Action*, pp. 199–214. Cambridge:Cambridge University Press.

Mayberry, Rachel I., and Elena Nicoladis. (2000). 'Gesture reflects language development: evidence from bilingual children', *Current Directions in Psychological Science*, 9/6: 192–96. DOI: 10.1111/1467-8721.00092

Maynard, Senko K. (1986). 'On back-channel behavior in Japanese and English casual conversation', *Linguistics*, 24/6. DOI: 10.1515/ling.1986.24.6.1079

Maynard, Senko K. (1987). 'Interactional functions of a nonverbal sign: Head movement in Japanese dyadic casual conversation', *Journal of Pragmatics*, 11/5: 589–606. DOI: 10.1016/0378-2166(87)90181-0

Mechraoui, Amal, and Faridah Noor Binti Mohd Noor. (2017). 'The direction giving pointing gestures of the Malay Malaysian speech community', *Gesture*, 16/1: 68–99. DOI: 10.1075/gest.16.1.03mec

Melinger, Alissa, and Willem J. M. Levelt. (2004). 'Gesture and the communicative intention of the speaker', *Gesture*, 4/2: 119–41. DOI: https://doi.org/10.1075/gest.4.2.02mel

Miklósi, Ádam, and Krisztina Soproni. (2006). 'A comparative analysis of animals' understanding of the human pointing gesture', *Animal Cognition*, 9/2: 81–93. DOI: 10.1007/s10071-005-0008-1

Miklósi, Áam, Péter Pongrácz, Gabriella Lakatos, József Topál, and Vilmos Csányi. (2005). 'A comparative study of the use of visual communicative signals in interactions between dogs (canis familiaris) and humans and cats (felis catus) and humans.', *Journal of Comparative Psychology*, 119/2: 179–86. DOI: 10.1037/0735-7036.119.2.179

Mittelberg, Irene. (2008). 'Peircean semiotics meets conceptual metaphor: Iconic modes in gestural representations of grammar'. Alan Cienki and Cornelia

Müller (eds), *Metaphor and Gesture*, pp. 115–54. Amsterdam: John Benjamins. DOI: 10.1075/gs.3.08mit

Mol, Lisette, Emiel Krahmer, and Mieke van de Sandt-Koenderman. (2013). 'Gesturing by speakers with aphasia: How does it compare?', *Journal of Speech, Language, and Hearing Research*, 56/4: 1224–36. DOI: 10.1044/1092-4388(2012/11-0159)

Morett, Laura M., Jennifer M. Roche, Scott H. Fraundorf, and James C. McPartland. (2020). 'Contrast is in the eye of the beholder: Infelicitous beat gesture increases cognitive load during online spoken discourse comprehension', *Cognitive Science*, 44/10: e12912. DOI: 10.1111/cogs.12912

Morgenstern, Aliyah, and Susan Goldin-Meadow (eds). (2021). *Gesture in Language: Development across the Lifespan. Language and the human lifespan.* Washington, DC: American Psychological Association.

Morris, D., P. Collet, P. Marsh, and M. O'Shaughnessy. (1979). *Gestures, their Origins and Distribution.* New York: Stein and Day.

Morris, Desmond. (1994). *Bodytalk: A World Guide to Gestures.* London: Jonathan Cape.

Morris, Desmond. (2019). *Postures: Body Language in Art.* London/New York: Thames & Hudson.

Müller, Cornelia. (1998). *Redebegleitende Gesten: Kulturgeschichte, Theorie, Sprachvergleich.* Berlin: Spitz.

Müller, Cornelia. (2002). 'A brief history of the origins of The International Society for Gesture Studies (ISGS)', *Gesture*, 2/1: 127–32. DOI: 10.1075/gest.2.1.11mul

Müller, Cornelia. (2008). 'What gestures reveal about the nature of metaphor'. Alan Cienki and Cornelia Müller (eds), *Metaphor and Gesture*, pp. 219–45. Amsterdam: John Benjamins. DOI: 10.1075/gs.3.12mul

Müller, Cornelia, Alan Cienki, Ellen Fricke, Silva Ladewig, David McNeill, and Sedinha Tessendorf (eds). (2013). *Body—Language—Communication: An International Handbook on Multimodality in Human Interaction*, Vol. 1. Berlin/Boston: De Gruyter. DOI: 10.1515/9783110261318

Müller, Cornelia, Alan J. Cienki, Ellen Fricke, Silva Ladewig, David McNeill, and Sedinha Tessendorf (eds). (2014). *Body—Language—Communication: An International Handbook on Multimodality in Human Communication.* Handbücher Zur Sprach- und Kommunikationswissenschaft/Handbooks of Linguistics and Communication Science (HSK) Ser., Vols 1-2, Vol. 2. Berlin: de Gruyter.

Neumann, Rognhild. (2004). 'The conventionalization of the Ring Gesture in German discourse'. Cornelia Müller and Roland Posner (eds), *The Semantics and Pragmatics of Everyday Gestures*, pp. 217–24. Weidler: Buchverlag.

Nicoladis, Elena, and Lisa Smithson. (2021). 'Gesture in bilingual language acquisition'. Aliyah Morgenstern and Susan Goldin-Meadow (eds), *Gesture in Language*, pp. 297–316. Washington DC/Berlin:APA/De Gruyter. DOI: 10.1515/9783110567526-012

Nishitani, N., and R. Hari. (2000). 'Temporal dynamics of cortical representation for action', *Proceedings of the National Academy of Sciences*, 97/2: 913–18. DOI: 10.1073/pnas.97.2.913

Núñez, Rafael. (2008). 'A fresh look at the foundations of mathematics: Gesture and the psychological reality of conceptual metaphor'. Alan Cienki and Cornelia Müller (eds), *Metaphor and Gesture*, pp. 93–114. Amsterdam: John Benjamins. DOI: 10.1075/gs.3.07nun

Núñez, Rafael, and E. Sweetser. (2006). 'With the future behind them: Convergent evidence from Ayamra language and gesture in the crosslinguistic comparison of spatial construal of time', *Cognitive Science*, 30: 401–50. DOI: 10.1207/s15516709cog0000_62

Núñez, Rafael, Kensy Cooperrider, D. Doan, and Jürg Wassmann. (2012). 'Contours of time: Topographic construals of past, present, and future in the Yupno valley of Papua New Guinea', *Cognition*, 124/1: 25–35. DOI: 10.1016/j.cognition.2012.03.007

Özçalışkan, Şeyda, and Nevena Dimitrova. (2013). 'How gesture input provides a helping hand to language development', *Seminars in Speech and Language*, 34/04: 227–36. DOI: 10.1055/s-0033-1353447

Özçalışkan, Şeyda, Ché Lucero, and Susan Goldin-Meadow. (2016). 'Is seeing gesture necessary to gesture like a native speaker?', *Psychological Science*, 27/5: 737–47. DOI: 10.1177/0956797616629931

Özyürek, Aslı. (2014). 'Hearing and seeing meaning in speech and gesture: Insights from brain and behaviour', *Philosophical Transactions of the Royal Society B: Biological Sciences*, 369/1651: 20130296. DOI: 10.1098/rstb.2013.0296

Özyürek, Aslı, Sotaro Kita, Shanley Allen, Reyhan Furman, and Amanda Brown. (2005). 'How does linguistic framing of events influence co-speech gestures?: Insights from crosslinguistic variation and similarities', *Gesture*, 5/1/2: 219–40. DOI: 10.1075/gest.5.1.15ozy

Özyürek, Aslı, Sotaro Kita, Shanley Allen, Amanda Brown, Reyhan Furman, and Tomoko Ishizuka. (2008). 'Development of cross-linguistic variation in speech and gesture: Motion events in English and Turkish', *Developmental Psychology*, 44/4: 1040–54. DOI: 10.1037/0012-1649.44.4.1040

Parrill, Fey. (2008). 'Form, meaning, and convention: A comparison of a metaphoric gesture with an emblem'. Alan J. Cienki and Cornelia Müller (eds), *Metaphor and Gesture*, pp. 195–217. Amsterdam/Philadelphia: John Benjamins.

Parrill, Fey. (2020). 'Using cognitive science to teach cognitive science: Embodied teaching and learning in the cognitive science classroom.', *Scholarship of Teaching and Learning in Psychology*, 9/1: 63–79. DOI: 10.1037/stl0000196

Pedelty, Laura Lee. (1987). 'Gesture in Aphasia' (PhD Thesis). The University of Chicago.

Poggi, Isabelle. (2011). 'Music and leadership: The choir conductor's multimodal communication'. Gale Stam and Mika Ishino (eds), *Integrating Gestures: The Interdisciplinary Nature of Gestures*, pp. 341–53. Amsterdam: John Benjamins.

Poizner, Howard, Edward S. Klima, and Ursula Bellugi. (2000). *What the Hands Reveal about the Brain*. Cambridge, MA: MIT Press.

Povinelli, Daniel, and D. Richard Davis. (1994). 'Differences Between Chimpanzees (Pan troglodytes) and Humans (Homo sapiens) in the Resting State of the Index Finger: Implications for Pointing', *Journal of Comparative Psychology*, 108/2: 134–9.

Raum, Otto Friedrich. (1973). *The Social Functions of Avoidances and Taboos among the Zulu*. Berlin/New York: de Gruyter.

Rauscher, Frances H., Robert M. Krauss, and Yihsiu Chen. (1996). 'Gesture, speech, and lexical access: The role of lexical movements in speech production', *Psychological Science*, 7/4: 226–31. DOI: 10.1111/j.1467-9280.1996.tb00364.x

Ricci Bitti, Pio E. (1992). 'Facial and manual components of Italian symbolic gestures'. Fernando Poyatos (ed.), *Advances in Nonverbal Communication*, pp. 187–96. Amsterdam/Philadelphia: John Benjamins.

Rimé, Bernard, Loris Schiaratura, Michel Hupet, and Anne Ghysselinckx. (1984). 'Effects of relative immobilization on the speaker's nonverbal behavior and on the dialogue imagery level', *Motivation and Emotion*, 8/4: 311–25. DOI: 10.1007/BF00991870

Rochat, Philippe. (1993). 'Hand–mouth coordination in the newborn: Morphology, determinants, and early development of a basic act', *Advances in Psychology*, 97: 265–88. DOI: 10.1016/S0166-4115(08)60956-5

Rohrer, Patrick L., Pilar Prieto, Elizabeth Delais-Roussarie, Sasha Calhoun, Poula Escudero, Marija Tabain, and Paul Warren. (2019). 'Beat gestures and prosodic domain marking in French'. *Proceedings of the 19th International Congress of Phonetic Sciences*, pp. 1500–04. Canberra, ACT: Australasian Speech Science and Technology Association Inc.

Rose, Miranda L. (2006). 'The utility of arm and hand gestures in the treatment of aphasia', *Advances in Speech Language Pathology*, 8/2: 92–109. DOI: 10.1080/14417040600657948

Rose, Miranda L. (2013). 'Releasing the constraints on aphasia therapy: The positive impact of gesture and multimodality treatments', *American Journal of Speech-Language Pathology*, 22/2. DOI: 10.1044/1058-0360(2012/12-0091)

Rowe, Meredith L., and Susan Goldin-Meadow. (2009). 'Early gesture *selectively* predicts later language learning', *Developmental Science*, 12/1: 182–87. DOI: 10.1111/j.1467-7687.2008.00764.x

Rowe, Meredith L., Ran Wei, and Virginia C. Salo. (2021). 'Early gesture predicts later language development'. Aliyah Morgenstern and Susan Goldin-Meadow (eds), *Gesture in Language*, pp. 93–112. Washington DC/Berlin:APA/De Gruyter:. DOI: 10.1515/9783110567526-004

Ruesch, Jurgen, and Weldon Kees. (1956). *Nonverbal Communication: Notes on the Visual Perception of Human Relations*. Berkeley, CA: University of California Press.

de Ruiter, Jan Peter. (2000). 'The production of gesture and speech'. David McNeill (ed.), *Language and Gesture*, pp. 284–311. Cambridge: Cambridge University Press.

de Ruiter, Jan Peter. (2007). 'Postcards from the mind: The relationship between speech, imagistic gesture, and thought', *Gesture*, 7/1: 21–38. DOI: 10.1075/gest.7.1.03rui

de Ruiter, Jan Peter, Ruth Breckinridge Church, Martha W. Alibali, and Spencer D. Kelly. (2017). 'The asymmetric redundancy of gesture and speech'. *Why Gesture?: How the Hands Function in Speaking, Thinking and Communicating*, pp. 59–75. Amsterdam: John Benjamins.

Saunders, E. Dale. (1985). *Mudrā: A Study of the Symbolic Gestures in Japanese Buddhist Sculpture*. Princeton: Princeton University Press.

Scahill, Rachael I., Chris Frost, Rhian Jenkins, Jennifer L. Whitwell, Martin N. Rossor, and Nick C. Fox. (2003). 'A longitudinal study of brain volume changes in normal aging using serial registered magnetic resonance imaging', *Archives of Neurology*, 60/7: 989. DOI: 10.1001/archneur.60.7.989

Schegloff, Emanuel A. (1984). 'On some gestures' relation to talk'. J. Maxwell Atkinson and John Heritage (eds), *Structures of Social Action: Studies in Conversation Analysis*, pp. 266–98. Cambridge/New York/Paris:Cambridge University Press.

Seidl, Ulrich, Ulrike Lueken, Philipp A. Thomann, Andreas Kruse, and Johannes Schröder. (2012). 'Facial expression in Alzheimer's disease: Impact of cognitive deficits and neuropsychiatric symptoms', *American Journal of Alzheimer's Disease & Other Dementias*, 27/2: 100–06. DOI: 10.1177/1533317512440495

Senghas, Ann, Sotaro Kita, and Asli Özyürek. (2004). 'Children creating core properties of language: Evidence from an emerging sign language in Nicaragua', *Science*, 305/5691: 1779–82. DOI: https://doi.org/10.1126/science.1100199

Shafto, Meredith A., and Lorraine K. Tyler. (2014). 'Language in the aging brain: The network dynamics of cognitive decline and preservation', *Science*, 346/6209: 583–87. DOI: 10.1126/science.1254404

Shepherd, Stephen. (2010). 'Following gaze: Gaze-following behavior as a window into social cognition', *Frontiers in Integrative Neuroscience*, 4: 5. DOI: 10.3389/fnint.2010.00005

Skubisz, Joanna. (2017). 'A systematic review of the methods reported in the journal GESTURE'. Presented at the iGesto conference, Porto, 2–3 February.

Sporer, Siegfried L., and Barbara Schwandt. (2007). 'Moderators of nonverbal indicators of deception: A meta-analytic synthesis', *Psychology, Public Policy, and Law*, 13/1: 1–34. DOI: 10.1037/1076-8971.13.1.1

Stam, Gale. (2017). 'Verb-framed, satellite-framed or in between?: A L2 learner's thinking for speaking in her L1 and L2 over 14 years'. Iraide Ibarretxe-Antuñano (ed.), *Human Cognitive Processing*, pp. 329–66. Amsterdam: John Benjamins. DOI: 10.1075/hcp.59.14sta

Stam, Gale, and Marion Tellier. (2021). 'Gesture helps second and foreign language learning and teaching'. Aliyah Morgenstern and Susan Goldin-Meadow (eds), *Gesture in Language*, pp. 335–64. Washington DC/Berlin:APA/De Gruyter. DOI: 10.1515/9783110567526-014

Stefanini, Silvia, Martina Recchia, and Maria Cristina Caselli. (2008). 'The relationship between spontaneous gesture production and spoken lexical ability in children with Down syndrome in a naming task', *Gesture*, 8/2: 197–218. DOI: 10.1075/gest.8.2.05ste

Streeck, Jurgen. (1994). 'Gesture as communication II: The audience as co-author', *Research on Language & Social Interaction*, 27/3: 239–67. DOI: 10.1207/s15327973rlsi2703_5

Sueyoshi, Ayano, and Debra M. Hardison. (2005). 'The role of gestures and facial cues in second language listening comprehension', *Language Learning*, 55/4: 661–99. DOI: 10.1111/j.0023-8333.2005.00320.x

Talmy, Leonard. (1985). 'Lexicalization patterns: Semantic structure in lexical forms'. Timothy Shopen (ed.), *Language Typology and Syntactic Description*, pp. 36–149. Cambridge: Cambridge University Press.

Teßendorf, Sedinha. (2014). 'Pragmatic and metaphoric gestures: Combining functional with cognitive approaches in the analysis of the brushing aside gesture'. Cornelia Müller, Silva Ladewig, Alan J. Cienki, Ellen Fricke, David McNeill, and Jana Bressem (eds), *Body—Language—Communication: An International Handbook on Multimodality in Human Interaction*, pp. 1540–58. De Gruyter Mouton: Berlin/Boston.

Tomasello, Michael. (2006). 'Why don't apes point?' Nicholas J. Enfield and Stephen C. Levinson (eds), *Roots of Human Sociality: Culture, Cognition and Interaction*, pp. 506–24. Oxford:Oxford University Press.

Tomasello, Michael, and Josep Call. (1997). *Primate Cognition*. New York: Oxford University Press.

Tomasello, Michael, and Josep Call. (2019). 'Thirty years of great ape gestures', *Animal Cognition*, 22/4: 461–9. DOI: 10.1007/s10071-018-1167-1

Torigoe, Takashi, and Wataru Takei. (2001). 'A descriptive analysis of early word combinations in deaf children's signed utterances', *Japanese Psychological Research*, 43/3: 156–61. DOI: 10.1111/1468-5884.00172

Trujillo, James P., Julija Vaitonyte, Irina Simanova, and Asli Özyürek. (2019). 'Toward the markerless and automatic analysis of kinematic features: A toolkit for gesture and movement research', *Behavior Research Methods*, 51/2: 769–77. DOI: 10.3758/s13428-018-1086-8

Trujillo, James, Asli Özyürek, Judith Holler, and Linda Drijvers. (2021). 'Speakers exhibit a multimodal Lombard effect in noise', *Scientific Reports*, 11/1: 16721. DOI: 10.1038/s41598-021-95791-0

Tylor, Edward Burnett. (1865). *Researches into the Early History of Mankind and the Development of Civilization*. Chicago: University of Chicago Press.

Unicode. (2023). 'Emoji frequency'. Retrieved 21 November 2023, from <https://home.unicode.org/emoji/emoji-frequency/>

Vainio, Lari. (2019). 'Connection between movements of mouth and hand: Perspectives on development and evolution of speech', *Neuroscience & Biobehavioral Reviews*, 100: 211–23. DOI: 10.1016/j.neubiorev.2019.03.005

Vajrabhaya, Prakaiwan, and Eric Pederson. (2018). 'Teasing apart listener-sensitivity: The role of interaction', *Gesture*, 17/1: 65–97. DOI: 10.1075/gest.00011.vaj

Wagner Cook, Susan. (2021). 'Understanding how gestures are produced and perceived'. Aliyah Morgenstern and Susan Goldin-Meadow (eds), *Gesture in Language*, pp. 243–68. Berlin: De Gruyter. DOI: 10.1515/9783110567526-010

Wilkins, David. (2003). 'Why pointing with the index finger is not a universal (in sociocultural and semiotic terms)'. Sotaro Kita (ed.), *Pointing: Where Language, Culture, and Cognition Meet*, pp. 171–215. Mahwah, NJ: L. Erlbaum Associates.

de Wit, Jan. (2022). 'I like the way you move: Robots that gesture, and their potential as second language tutors for children' (PhD Thesis). Tilburg University.

Wu, Shengwang, Zhongmin Li, Shiji Li, Qiang Liu, and Weiyu Wu. (2023). 'An overview of gesture recognition'. Vijayakumar Varadarajan, Jerry Chun-Wei Lin, and Pascal Lorenz (eds), International Conference on Computer Application and Information Security (ICCAIS 2022), p. 52. DOI: 10.1117/12.2671842

Wu, Ying Choon, and Seana Coulson. (2011). 'Are depictive gestures like pictures? Commonalities and differences in semantic processing', *Brain and Language*, 119/3: 184–95. DOI: 10.1016/j.bandl.2011.07.002

Wundt, Wilhelm. (1900). *The Language of Gestures*. Berlin/New York: De Gruyter Mouton.

Xu, Jiang, Patrick. J. Gannon, Karen Emmorey, Jason F. Smith, and Allen R. Braun. (2009). 'Symbolic gestures and spoken language are processed by a common neural system', *Proceedings of the National Academy of Sciences*, 106/49: 20664–69. DOI: 10.1073/pnas.0909197106

Yap, De Fu, Geoffrey Brookshire, and Daniel Casasanto. (2018). 'Beat gestures encode spatial semantics'. *Proceedings of the 40th Annual Meeting of the Cognitive Science Society, CogSci 2018, Madison, WI, USA, 25–28 July, 2018*, p. 1211. Austin, TX: Cognitive Science Society.

Index